CAGED NO MORE

Wisdom From Women Who Broke Free From Societal Constraints

SANCTUARY PUBLISHING

Copyright ©2021 Sanctuary Publishing

All Rights Reserved. Apart from any fair dealing for the purposes of research or private study, or criticism or review, as permitted under the Copyright, Designs and Patents act 1988, this publication may only be reproduced, stored or transmitted, in any form or by any means, with the prior permission in writing of the copyright owner, or in the case of the reprographic reproduction in accordance with the terms of licensees issued by the Copyright Licensing Agency. Enquiries concerning reproduction outside those terms should be sent to the publisher.

TABLE OF CONTENTS

Introduction 1

1. **Allison Haynes** 2
   "She Said WHAT?"
   About the Author 8
2. **Claire Bradshaw** 9
   Awakening From the Trance
   About the Author 18
3. **Annamaya Ananda** 19
   Awakening From the Trance
   About the Author 26
4. **Denise Marshall** 27
   Dare To Look Within, Set Yourself Free
   About the Author 33
5. **Holly Lo** 34
   The Message in The Mess
   About the Author 40
6. **Jeannie Lynch** 41
   Ila's Moon
   About the Author 48
7. **Jennifer Bertone** 49
   Birthing A Goddess
   About the Author 54

8.	**Judy Lynn Mitchell**	55
	When Your Soul Speaks... Listen	
	About the Author	62
9.	**Lisa Évoluer**	64
	From The Superficial Advertising World to Spiritual Freedom	
	About the Author	71
10.	**Mathilde Anglade**	72
	Daring To Be Great, Or A Story on Choice & Belief Using Land as A Portal	
	About the Author	79
11.	**Phoebe Leona**	80
	A Story of Co-Creation with Chaos	
	About the Author	86
12.	**Roxy Sewell**	87
	Her Inner Labyrinth	
	About the Author	93
13.	**Sarah Collins**	94
	The Answer Has Always Been You	
	About the Author	101
14.	**Stacy Johnston**	102
	Underneath The Music	
	About the Author	108
15.	**Suzanne Wing**	109
	The Journey to Living Wildly Peaceful	
	About the Author	114
16.	**Vanessa Parrado**	115
	You Were Born Free	
	About the Author	122

INTRODUCTION

There are too many external pressures telling us the "right" way and the "wrong" way to live in this lifetime. These have been turned into societal norms or constraints.

Societal constraints aren't "bad"...

But when societal constraints restrict you from seeing the brilliance, abundance and joy that is your true nature, something needs to shift. These norms turn into pressures that box you in from seeing what is possible for your reality. You no longer trust yourself; you rely on external support to tell you what you can and can not do.

This takes your power away from you. The intuition gets pushed aside, and the status quo is followed. And when we feel the desire to shift, we get stuck because we have never relied on ourselves before. Following the norm has created a false sense of safety around us, and stepping out of the norm means stepping into the unknown.

The unknown doesn't have to be scary, anxiety-ridden and all-consuming. We are always playing with the unknown whether we follow societal constraints or not. Caged No More is an expression of courage, resiliency and self-trust.

Allow these stories to be the beginning of trusting yourself and your wildest dreams because truly anything is possible; we just limit ourselves.

May these women show you that it is safe to take the leap and bet on yourself.
May these women shine light on how magical life can be even after the depths of pain.
May these women guide you on your path of becoming Caged No More.

Annette Maria Szproch

ALLISON HAYNES

"SHE SAID WHAT?"

I've been sitting here thinking about what it means not to be caged anymore by societal expectations. It got me stuck. What was the moment that made me realise I was caged? What was the moment I opened the door to my cage and flew free? And then I realised it wasn't ONE moment, but an unfolding of events and small steps. It was looking back and realising how far I had come, what the journey looked like, and in looking back, helped me to look forward and plan a more value-based journey. In that slow unfolding and those small moments, there were three larger turning points, I think of as pivotal moments, that have defined who I am now and where I am headed. Two of them intertwine and are difficult to separate but are distinct from each other. I find it interesting that, reflecting on the earlier moments, after having gone through the later ones, I now view them differently from how I did at the time.

My "normal" seemed so good to outsiders. We were the traditional nuclear family of the 80s: Mum, Dad, two kids, and a cat. Dad worked in a blue-collar job and eventually moved up to white-collar management. Mum was the quintessential stay-at-home mum, making clothes and baking cookies. My younger sister and I were smart, pretty and had friends. We had extracurricular activities and wanted for nothing. I was happy in primary school—or so I thought. Looking back now, I wasn't happy at all; I was "masking". I was desperately trying to keep my mother happy so she did not invalidate me. Then we moved.

The move to another state was not a success. While my dad got a better job that made us much more financially secure, Mum was not happy, and went back to work due to loneliness. I was too smart for the year level that my age determined, so I was moved up a grade—big mistake. Not only was I an outcast because I was the new girl, but I was also the outcast because I was smart and because I was young. I do not remember a day going by without being bullied, taunted, left out or sidelined. But, through all that, there was something more, something I could not, at the time, put my finger on. Why was it that all my attempts to fit in failed? Why was it that the other kids seemed to have it so much easier? Why did they get the difference between when a comment was sarcasm or just downright mean? I coped by becoming very passive, working hard, and therefore ostracising myself even more. "Teacher's pet", "goody two shoes", "Pizza face (due to my bad acne)". I became so distressed that it culminated in three suicide attempts. My parents are still unaware to this day that I tried to take my own life.

Uni was not much different, although there was no bullying. But still, the feeling of "not quite" fitting in persisted. I did well academically, but not as well as I thought I should be doing. I was gifted, so why was the work so hard to get done? I ended up walking out of my Master's degree.

This theme of feeling "not quite" continued through my marriage, having my kids, and trying to advocate for them. Both my kids are autistic and ADHD, and that in itself created a lot of stress. When they were diagnosed, the prevailing narrative was to get autistics to look and behave more "normally". To fit in. To mask. To suppress and ignore their authentic selves. I'm sure you can see what the fallout from that would be. Unfortunately, they now also have PTSD, something I am determined that my clients do not end up with.

Eventually, my marriage fell apart. It was no big drama, we stayed amicable, we had been not much more than friends for the previous few years, and we recognised that it had just seen its day. So, we parted ways.

So, at forty, with a brand-new psychology degree, I was single. Now what? Short term, my focus was on making enough money to get by, but after a year, I was at the point where I needed to address this feeling of "not quite". There was also a clear and distinct lack of love for myself. I did not like myself. I was disgusted at some of my behaviours but had no idea how to change them. And so, I entered therapy.

That was the moment—the moment Pandora's box opened, and change started. I was sitting in my therapist's room about halfway through my session. I mentioned something my mother had said to me when I was a child; I can't even remember what she said. My therapist, usually so calm, collected and not one to react to grand statements, pulled back, grimaced and said those words: "She said WHAT?". I repeated them. She then said, "that is NOT OK".

What was so surprising was not that it was inappropriate, but that I had absolutely no idea that it was so hurtful. To me, that's what mothers said. That is why I still can't remember what it was my therapist reacted to so intensely. It was my normal. But if that was not normal, then what was?

We dug deep and explored together. I discovered that I had trauma, not from the stress of raising my kids, as I thought, but from the experience of not having my emotional needs met as a child. From the outside, our family was "perfect", conforming to middle-class societal expectations. I knew it wasn't, my mother was clearly anxious, but I had no idea that what had happened was essentially emotional neglect. Gaining love from my mother was conditional on portraying the "perfect daughter", smart, well behaved, in agreeance with her beliefs and values, which very much aligned with those of the community we mixed with. It was subtle, oh so subtle, and no one suspected a thing as there was no physical abuse or neglect. Comments such as "That dress looks nice, it hides your fat legs" and "what happened to the other 5%" were a normal part of our discourse.

I was born a quiet, naturally self-content baby, so this treatment from my mother exacerbated this and turned me into a repressed, suicidal teen. I remember so clearly sitting on our back step, crying, and berating myself for being so ungrateful. It got worse; I felt that I was so unhappy but could not see why. Therefore that meant that I must have been the problem. So, I thought, let's remove the problem. Let's stop the bullying. Let's stop the stress I cause others. Let's get out of here. Luckily, I failed.

I remember clearly a session with my therapist. She had suggested a values exercise, so I could determine what my core values were. She had an interesting approach to this. After the initial values sort into "yes/maybe" and "no", she used a Jungian approach by directing me to lay them out how they made sense to me. I was so surprised at how that fell out. I had two clear sets of values, with a clear gap between the two sets. On the left were the values I was currently living by, which included status, image, financial success, knowledge, intelligence. On the right were the values that I wanted to live by: honesty, compassion, empathy, connection, authenticity. I looked at the two sets of values, and with a bit of prompting, it came to me. On the left side were my mothers' values, and by trying to live by them, I was trying to be like my mother, and therefore trying to earn her love. Her voice was in my head every moment of the day, dictating how I should act, think and feel. How I should "be".

From that moment, I began the journey to find my authentic self, and with the support of my therapist, I was able to mainly put aside my mother's voice and start to build my own identity. To say this was easy would be a lie. It was confronting. I had to keep reminding myself that this pain, this raw vulnerability, this change, this feeling of being untethered, was all for a reason. But, boy oh, boy, did it hurt at times. Eventually, I learned to trust my own idea of what authentic and valued living was and started to lean into my own values. The path was rocky, but eventually, I began to like myself. I started to realise that I had traits that I had suppressed to try to please my mother—and my husband—but that I felt were inherently who I was. Compassion was the top value, and being able to lean into this allowed me to care for others, show my emotions more genuinely, and make me better at what I do for my career. I learned to self-validate rather than gain validation from others, and this new confidence looked quieter, calmer and somehow, stronger.

Unfortunately, this created a lot of broken friendships and relationships along the way. People who were used to me jumping to their aid started to call me selfish. People who were used to me keeping friendships alive started to call me hard work. This made me question, "Am I?" Am I selfish? Am I hard work? My internal narrative from birth validated that. I had to sit with that distress and keep re-assessing what was actually going on. And finally, I was able to answer, "NO!" I was not selfish or hard work. I was healthy, and the people that could not handle that were the ones that sucked my energy and did not give back. I was able to release those relationships and value myself finally. What it did build was a more secure sense of self and an ability to start to set healthy boundaries. It helped me to recognise what was actually important for my well-being and what was just trying to please others in the desperate attempt to keep everything smooth and free of conflict. Most of us know that it is a lost cause; there is always someone not happy! I learnt to be OK with other people not being OK.

I walked out of therapy feeling "fixed". I felt reborn, and very much aligned with the story of the phoenix, my authentic self, rising out of the ashes of my false self. I even had a phoenix tattooed on my back to celebrate the "new me". I went out into the world with a new purpose and new energy.

But.

But it didn't quite work. There was something still missing. Why was it that, if I was so healthy now and so good at knowing who I was, I kept slipping into unhealthy romantic relationships? Why was it that I still felt like an outsider in social events? Why did I find it so hard to understand others, and miss innuendo, and take things so literally? Why was I working much less than my peers but was so burnt out? Why was organising myself and finishing things almost impossible for me? Why did I keep seeing easy answers in things that others did not even seem to consider?

Why was I still so different?

Then I met someone. He was the catalyst to another great change, both positive and negative. This change is still very new, very fresh, and I am still processing, and is entwined with another self-realisation.

I thought I had met my soulmate, and for the first year or so, that certainly was my experience. He helped me to really lean into who I was and to recognise that I could do more with my career than what I was currently doing. During this part of our relationship, I started to really "watch" myself and became very curious about what he saw when he looked at me. At that time, he did not see the disorganised, emotionally fragile, vulnerable, burnt-out but intelligent psychologist that I saw. He saw a ditzy, playful, clumsy, but strong, fierce, and quirky businesswoman. I liked what he saw, and I accepted and internalised those traits in myself and used them to balance the fierce independence I had developed. I saw them as my panther and my kitten—two separate but linked parts of my whole, two sides that balanced each other. So, I decided to trust this version and open my own clinic.

At the same time, it finally became clear. That feeling of "not quite"? It was not because I was broken, or traumatised, or stupid, or weak. It was because I was autistic. It was because I was also ADHD. When I finally asked someone who I really trusted, "do you think I might be autistic?" the response was, "You finally worked that out, did you?"

So, again, I started down the new rabbit hole of personal identity. I also had to work out where I fit in the world, as it certainly wasn't following neurotypical expectations! Once again, I entered therapy to help this process.

What did it mean to own this label of "autistic and ADHD"? Certainly, there was stigma as it is generally seen as a disability. But was it really? My business, which supports autistics and others that identify as "left of centre", certainly does not see it that way. I had to work through my own internalised ableism about my real thoughts. There were some great moments and some horrible ones.

One of the best moments was being prescribed stimulant medication for ADHD. I clearly remember the day I took the first dose. I was so nervous! This was basically a form of Meth, a horribly disabling street drug, and I was about to willingly subject my body to this. It took about half an hour of looking at that little white tablet in my hand before I could take it.

I shouldn't have worried. It was totally life-changing in all positive ways. I could think clearly; I could concentrate; I could sit still; I could remember things; I could track conversations better; I could control my impulsivity. I felt smarter. I finally felt like all those amazing ideas and thoughts that circled my brain every minute of the day could be realised and made concrete. I was thinking, "I could really make a difference in the autistic space now." I was so excited and ready to take on a million projects, knowing that I could finish them this time.

This realisation and clarity allowed me to dive deeply into what it meant to be autistic in this intolerant world. I became outspoken for my kind, what we call neurokin. I was simultaneously putting myself and my views right on the edge of accepted society but feeling the most accepted and safe that I had ever felt. This feeling of belonging, and connection, was new and comforting. However, it was also scary as it was an opportunity to lean on others a little, to allow myself to be vulnerable, and to gain authentic support. It challenged my feelings of independence. Slowly, I learnt that connection—true, authentic connection—was enriching and helpful. It did not mean I was weak; in contrast, I was strong in recognising when I needed support and asking for it.

However, along with this, there was the lowest moment of my life so far. The lifting brain fog also lifted my confusion about my relationship. It had started on a high, an instant meeting of soulmates. The deep connection that comes when someone SEES you. I felt that finally, I had met someone that could enrich my life while I enriched his. We could both be better as a result of being together. He was the one that made me see I was good enough to open my business. Within six weeks of meeting, he moved in.

However, we faced some challenges. We had to suddenly take on full custody of his two young children and sort schools, support and living space for them. This put his studies under pressure. Then there seemed to be a string of "challenges" that stopped him from moving forward. Mediation, no licence, inability to find a job, lacking direction in life, visitations resuming. I threw all of my resources at this and supported him and his kids as much as I possibly could—emotionally, physically and financially.

I noticed that it impacted the way we related to each other and caused tension and some resentments. I noticed that I had started to "walk on eggshells" and that after each argument, I walked away feeling like it was all my fault and feeling like I hadn't been heard properly. This niggling unease grew.

Then I started meds, and the scales dropped from my eyes. I had been gaslighted, manipulated and used. My partner was psychologically abusive, and I was, in fact, in a DV relationship. So, I had to break it off. The fallout, the fear, the trauma is still happening as I write this.

But.

But this time, I know who I am. I know where I fit. I know my resilience and strength. Yes, I am traumatised, but I now know that the people around me are good and are my neurokin, and I feel uplifted, seen and supported by them. I hurt now. Deeply. But I will heal. This time I know this, as I have better insight, better knowledge and feel free for the first time in my life. Free to be me, free to live to my values, and free to fulfil my passion.

Free.

ABOUT THE AUTHOR
ALLISON HAYNES

Allison Haynes is an Autistic/ADHD psychologist who runs and owns Left of Centre Therapies, a neurodiversity affirmative therapy clinic that supports individuals who feel they don't "fit" in our neurotypical society. The majority of her staff are neurodivergent (autistic, ADHD, or just a bit left of centre). She is the mother of two autistic, gender-fluid children, and her experience with parenting her amazing children led her to study psychology and open her clinic. She is also a speaker, supervisor, published author and lobbyist for education and disability.

Allison's passion is to see every person accepted for who they are, for neurodivergence to be removed from the disability and medical paradigm and accepted as just a wonderful variant of human existence.

Website: http://www.loctherapies.com
Facebook: https://www.facebook.com/LOCTherapies
Instagram: https://www.instagram.com/loctherapies
LinkedIn: https://www.linkedin.com/company/left-of-centre-therapies/

ANNAMAYA ANANDA

9 SECRETS FOR STAYING IN YOUR PERSONAL POWER

"God's GIFT to you is, the WISDOM gained through travelling along the tunnel of the light and tunnel of the dark" Annamaya

so please know this from my SOULFUL heart to yours...
(you beautiful radiant woman reading this passage)

"You are Thine and YOUR SOUL is pure MAGIC. Time to SPRINKLE your MAGIC on the world" - Annamaya

As an ambitious, talented, over-achiever I spent my twenties excelling in sport, university, and career. I had the golden touch with everything I wanted to have, do, or be. Things I wanted, I almost always got. I'm sure I somehow got coded with an encryption for a determined mind and courageous heart as I have always been brave enough to fully embrace everything I set my mind on.

My drive and self-motivation were awakened in me from a young age. My dad had me listening to Zig Ziglar and he posted motivational quotes on my bedroom walls. But it took me years to discover my tenacity and drive allowed me to hold things together and commit to goals no matter what.

In October 2013, at the age of 33, I was diagnosed with the autoimmune disease hypothyroidism, then a week later found out I was pregnant with our second son. When I told my boss, I was given a 'redundancy' the night before our first family holiday in almost two years. "How can you do your job if pregnant?" my employer said. So my pregnancy was spent fighting and winning an unfair dismissal case which settled the month before my son was born in March 2014.

By the next month, another blow fell. Diagnosed with Hashimoto's and adrenal fatigue, I was bedridden for 18 hours of the day for most of the year, while coming to terms with a trial separation from my children's father. My emotional and physical health suffered under the illness and the relationship breakdown with the man I thought would always be by my side.

If 2014 wasn't bad enough, 2015 saw me go from bad to worse in every area of my life.

At the start of that year I realised during my first kundalini experience that my efforts to heal relationships had failed. All I could focus on was me and my healing journey. Whatever lay ahead, I was now not prepared to ignore my emotions or suppress my pain or power. I wouldn't dim my light anymore for anyone.

That resolution was tested a month later when a phone call with my father saw my last pillar of family support crumble. He had always been my rock, but told me his wife, my stepmother, had told him to choose between her or me. He chose her. My world dropped into anger and rage that he could not find a courageous way to have both of us in his life and was bowing to his wife's insecurities. It was devastating to be suddenly abandoned by a man who had centred his life around his daughters—he raised us a single dad—was devastating.

By late March a series of mystical events happened after a full moon ceremony and past life regression session where I realised that I had no memories at all under 12. But the universe had a different plan for me to understand these years, to unpack forgotten trauma and pain.

Over two weeks, God delivered to me out of nowhere three significant women (individually coming to me) from my childhood to fill in my memory gap. What they told me triggered a nervous breakdown where I had no idea of what really my life was or what truth to believe.

By now my kids' father temporarily moved back in and was even more emotionally and mentally cruel than before. Unable to hold or support me, he would instead yell abuse.

It was challenging. I felt very unprotected and scared despite having all the things society says are important—home, investments, savings, kids, partner. It felt more a nightmare than a dream life.

Within six weeks things had turned around. I found a spiritual guru in India and attended a one day workshop that for the first time in my life let me cry out all the pain. In a place I didn't know, a place of complete non-judgement, I released a lifetime of pain. A life filled with fear of rejection, abandonment, feeling unlovable and of not being able to be me. It was in this moment that I chose to declare the very things I wanted for my life.

But before I could start healing my wounds I had to lose everything I had built my life on- people, loved ones, family, illusions.

I had to learn to build the foundations of my future self from these new truths about who I truly am, who I want to be and what I want for my life.

Following that path with this spiritual guru from India for over four years was the sole reason I have come out as I am. It was able to make sense of the chaos and help explain my inner and outer turmoil. I truly chose to learn and embrace how this ancient wisdom from the east could give me context of how to live my most powerful self in the challenges of the modern world.

This path was my biggest teacher. It gave me the strength to go headfirst in to battle for what mattered to me most, my children.

During a long and traumatic custody battle, I was forced to defend my sanity and ability to parent. I had to defend many lies about me through a court system where my kids' father decided he wanted to refuse me rights to my children based on how I was living life.

For months before I took the stand in court my stomach was in knots. Yet on the day God had better plans for me. What erupted was my power to defend and stand authentically for me despite the eyes of hate against me. I truly believe now that it is not until you are backed into a corner that you realise your true power. Pain persisted right until the end when the judge said I was a perfectly good, positive mother who was not inflicting my spiritual beliefs on my children.

The amount of pain that I endured from past friends or family, I would never wish that on anyone. I knew I would never end my life, but I can see how easily with no support someone could choose that decision.

My understanding of loved ones having your back became messed up. I had supposed friends betray me and allow my ex to trespass through my home. It broke and violated every sense of trust, privacy and support I had in friends, loved ones, family and authority figures.

What was hurtful was never once was anyone answerable for their actions or lies. I could not believe in the injustice of it all.

For years during dark moments, I would lie under my doona afraid and scared of the world, hoping the floor would open and something would come and take me away from it all. That hole never came but somehow I kept choosing the baby steps to keep consciously working on me.

When so many understandably numb their pain with an addiction or negative influence, I chose to get healthy physically, mentally, emotionally, and spiritually. I fully embraced how to find my resilience from within. How to strengthen my mind, body, and soul through practicing fasting, enemas, daily practice, spiritual routine, motivational mentors, meditation, coaching to constantly unpack trauma and choose life.

I never forced anyone to think or believe in what I did. I chose to focus living each day in a way that could help or heal me. I chose despite it all to stand as me authentically every day, knowing that justice and truth would one day come.

It was *8 years* of enduring the toughest years for my heart. I healed that heart and my life piece by piece by choosing an intentional life and to offer service to others while taking responsibility for my emotional state.

What I learned about life was to not find a way to escape the fires of life, but to find a way to stand in the fires and not get burned.

To find a way to stand in the ring and be a fighter.

To find a way to not avoid the storm, but be calm during the storm.

This is only some of my story and thank you for being here with me along the way.

I am Annamaya.

I am the nourishment I want to give to souls struggling like I was, who are ready to commit to a better future.

I am a passionate woman who has activated a warrior heart with a thirst to stand for a new way of being. A new way of living life powerfully no matter what it presents you on the outside.

I am inspired to take a stand, as I see so many women who have lost their feminine power, that essence of who they truly are as their magnetic self where life is drawn to you and things come to you as a vibrational match.

A Dame spirit (the feminine of the king spirit) where she stands charismatically, energetically, and powerfully in her warrior, grounded truth.

I believe in truly wanting to help share what worked for me. I feel so grateful to be able to share the daily practices that helped every part of my journey across every part of my life.

Annamaya's Nine Sacred Secrets Staying in Your Personal Power

1. **CONNECTION (to help you stay grounded)**
   Every single day take time connect to the Divine
   (God, source, universe etc)
2. **MEDITATION (to stay emotionally balanced)**
   Upon waking and last thing before sleep
3. **SELF TALK (to control and influence how you think, act, behave)**
   - Choose to be fully responsible for what you say to yourself.
   - What can help you—podcasts, writing a letter to your future self, journaling, time in nature, singing out loud, ecstatic dancing to get into your body and out of your head, creative play.
4. **EMOTIONAL AWARENESS (accept and recognise ALL emotions are real and valid)**
   Your intuition is your greatest guide. There are
   two approaches you can consider you may need:
   - READ THE ENERGY—what's REALLY going on
     1. Know what conversations to have (even if feeling vulnerable, uncertain, or scared)
     2. Know what conversations not to have.
   - JOURNALING EXERCISE: (in a quiet place to ask yourself what is really going on)
     - What am I feeling right now?
     - Where am I feeling it in my body?
     - When was the earliest memory of this feeling?
     - What did I most need at the time?
     - What was most missing in that moment?
     - What did I most long for back then?
     - How can I give this to myself right now?
     - Then choose one of releasing rituals below to let it go
5. **STRENGTHEN YOUR NERVOUS SYSTEM (increase your resilience to withstand life and any uncomfortable experiences)**
   - Choose fasting and enemas (break emotional patterns stored in food)
   - Cryotherapy,
   - Frequency therapy (super effective way to influence of energetic state)
6. **REMOVE TOXICITY (remove what is toxic to you)**

All negative energy is bad for you (emotional, mental, spiritual, physical):
- Food (plant based living food over chemical laden processed 'dead' food);
- Chemicals (from food, house cleaning products, makeup etc);
- Water (instal filter system in your home, high vibration water only);
- People – anyone that makes you feel less of who you are (remove people that bring anger, rage, drama, abuse, toxic energy);
- Spiritually – remove things like mainstream media, porn, horror movies.

7. **UNPACK YOUR TRAUMA (suffering is when you keep repeating painful experiences. This will liberate yourself of emotional triggers, and to stop repeating painful cycles)**

    Find a quiet place and journal out your responses to these questions:
    - When you explore your body, where do you feel this in you?
    - What belief or thought were you telling yourself during that experience? ie why did they do it to me?
    - What is the opposite of this thought? ie what if this was not about me and about them
    - Is there any chance of that opposite thought being true?
    - How has this strengthened me now?

8. **TOP SIX VALUES IN YOUR WHEEL OF LIFE (every three-six months determine what are the most important values across all areas of your life)**

    Your Wheel of life is made of Eight Areas of Life

Step 1: WHEEL OF LIFE DIAGRAM
Using the blank wheel of life diagram below answer these questions for each of the eight areas (each pie of the circle) shown above:
1. What are your top six values for this area?
    - Example: Family and Friends Area of Life: top six values could be connection, openness, trust, love, kindness, respect
2. With each of these listed six values, now rank from top value #1 to least high value #
    - Example: Family and Friends Area of Life: top six values in order could be

1. Unwavering Love (has your back and expression of love)
2. Connection (close bond, support, vulnerable, judgement free)
3. Openness (willingness to share)
4. Trust (can confide in them)
5. Kindness (treat you with thought and care)
6. Respect (accepts your fully despite choices, beliefs, opinions, lifestyle)

3. Now complete this for each of the six Areas of the Wheel of Life

Step 2: INTEGRATION & EMBODIMENT (so you live your life Intentionally to your top values)
- What would life look like if you lived intentionally to your values?
- How would that happen or now not be happening?
    Example: Health & Wellness
    (one area from wheel of life)
- I would eat nourishing food,
- I would be checking in with what I say to myself when I make food choices
- I will plan my week of food and meals so I don't get caught out or eat bad choices when hungry

9. **RELEASING RITUALS (how to handover to God and let go)**
    - *FIRE RITUAL:* write out on paper what you want to create, what you want to let go of, what you want to handover to. Now burn your papers and handover those desires to God
    - *LOVE LETTER TO GOD:* write a letter that details out your wishes to God
    - *PRAYER:* the Hoponopono prayer,
    - **FORGIVENESS EXERCISE**—write a letter to the person you want to forgive then burn it and hand over the rest to God
    - *GRATITUDE*—daily write out 10 reasons why you are grateful today

To awaken your power is not some magic pill, potion or person. It's about addressing the core of who you are, what you stand for, where your passion lies, what the point of you being here in this world is ... and when you start to find clarity in these answers a whole new awakening happens.

All of a sudden there's an inspired drive, you wake up ready to take on the world and there's an energy, even magnetism, about you that you can't hide from.

It radiates from your very essence, a flow about you, a receptivity that has you drawing life to you not away from you, where you show up in your fullest, most authentic expression of who you truly are, the light and the shade and own it all. And here you are with passion, purpose and influencing the world with your high energy and vitality.

In the chapter I have shared only a small snippet of what I have been through, yet it's enough to share the last eight years of what I needed to find me. The real feminine power that I have always had in me, but wouldn't dare express or embody. Who I am didn't come easily or without resistance.

I seemed to have always chosen the right path. Not the easy path. And with that has come a lot of facing up to myself and others in ways that made me think at times I was crazy for putting myself in these rings of fire, but part of me also knew that I am not here to dim my light for anyone else anymore. I am here to shine my genius and show others how to step into and stay in your personal power.

Next Steps

In my life I had to let go of the foundations built on the illusions of pain, trauma, abandonment and chaos, and realise that nothing of my past painful experiences was here to cause me fall short of who I truly am. That I have been given each of these opportunities—as chaotic and at times unbearably painful experiences as they were—were a catalyst and means for me to find myself and my personal power. There to awaken my magic and gifts to the world.

On my journey of finding who I truly am I have found many women who have lost their way, their power and who they truly are just like I had. If you are like I was this is the right place for your personal transformation.

My promise is to give you the tools and top resources you can use to step into and stay in your personal power, no matter what life throws at you.

My desire is to truly help you stay in your personal power as you up-level your business or personal life. Both are intrinsically connected and I'm here to help you up-level to the next version of you waiting on the other side of my coaching containers.

I use a combination of womb-like safe containers and frequency therapy to awaken your dormant yet powerful life force within so you can live a life of freedom, joy and liberation.

Your Personal Power is showing up in life knowing you can withstand anything personally or professionally.

xox

Much love and power from 'The Soul Nourisher'

And recognised globally as 'Annamaya'.

I love connecting with others. Reach out by my website or social media platforms so I can support you in your personal or business quest, and you can learn to step into and stay in your personal power as life happens for you.

ABOUT THE AUTHOR
ANNAMAYA ANANDA

A golden girl in her twenties—ambitious, talented, great at sport, academia and in her career. Then her 'perfect' world completely fell apart. Eight years of intense emotional and mental plan, where she withstood lies, injustices, betrayal, greed and manipulation. Yet she chose to fight through consciously to help heal and rebuild her life.

With qualifications in Master's of Business Administration, Commerce, Business (HR), Photography, Life Coaching, Presenting, NLP and Writing whilst also attending 40+ spiritual programs by Life Bliss University (India).

An international business consultant, mentor, multi-business owner, facilitator, host, speaker and coach with three interview series (65,000 views organically via Facebook and creator of high impact communities online called Global Frequency Movement and Global Frequency Collective

Her specialty: Helping you Stay in Your Personal Power as you commit to uplevelling your life.

What she offers: Either a one on one personal immersion experience with limited intakes annually by application or by partnering with her in her affiliated opportunities: frequency therapy, crypto or high-vibe water.

Website: http://www.iamannamaya.com
Facebook: https://www.facebook.com/annamaya.ananda
Instagram: https://www.instagram.com/iamannamaya
Email: hello@iamannamaya.com

CLAIRE BRADSHAW

AWAKENING FROM THE TRANCE

It was 2010, I was thirty-one and living in Melbourne, Australia. I was working in my 'dream' role —a career that had taken me many twists and turns to finally arrive at. I had bought an apartment and had a great relationship, friends, money for holidays, clothes, and savings. I had all the things that society deems as 'successful'. But I felt far from having 'made it'. I felt empty inside. I was sick. I was tired. I was bored. I didn't want to live in a big part of the life I had created. But I had no idea how to get out of it.

I had so many swirling thoughts and emotions running around. I felt cheated and angry, as if I'd been unfairly sold a dream that didn't materialise. I felt confused and empty, not knowing what to do next. I also felt this deep guilt for feeling this way. 'I mean, how ungrateful was I?' So, in response to this big internal muddle, I pushed down the feelings and kept moving forward. This was until my body said a big solid 'NO' and forced me to stop and look inside.

For the previous few years, I'd worked feverishly to get a position in marketing for big multinational brands. I worked long hours, tried to play the corporate games and in turn enjoyed the glitz and glamour of advertising parties and corporate events. I thought this was it; I was proving to myself that I was successful and that my parents would finally be proud of my achievements.

I grew up in the south of England in a family that highly valued education and grades. Some of my earliest memories were of getting care bear toys for good grades at school. I felt loved and accepted when I achieved, and I now realise that it drove me to become addicted to achievement and validation.

So many of my childhood memories are of me working for hours at my desk. I'll never forget being told my predicted grades for GCSE exams were C's and D's when my parents returned from a parent-teacher meeting. I could see the disappointment on their faces. I felt the sinking feeling in my gut and felt like I was letting them down. Perhaps, I just wasn't good enough, I thought.

And in that moment, something fired within me. I would prove to everyone in the family that I was good enough and was deserving enough. But little did I know that this need to 'prove' something to be loved and accepted would cause me a whole lot of pain later on.

So going back to that office job in 2010. Over the previous year or so, I'd been getting frequently ill—colds and viruses, skin rashes, nausea, IBS symptoms, headaches. It had been one thing after another. And then that year, I got diagnosed with hypoglycemia and would feel constantly weak and wobbly. It wasn't until I started getting vertigo symptoms that things got much worse. I'd be doing a presentation at work, and then the room would begin to spin, or I'd be walking along a corridor and then feel as though the ground dropped away. Some days it was so bad that I couldn't get out of bed. And then the anxiety came; I never knew when the dizzy spells would arrive, so I became super cautious about accepting invitations to events. It was debilitating, and my confidence levels plummeted.

I was going down, fast. I'd visited many doctors over the previous year, but it wasn't until 2010 that I found a doctor who looked straight into my eyes and said, 'everything is ok. We'll get you better'. For the first time in my life, I felt fully seen, heard, and validated. I felt safe. He conducted a bunch of tests that thankfully came back negative. And then he said that the only thing he could do was give me some pills to manage the dizzy spells when they arose. I took the script. But there was an intuitive voice within me that said, 'don't take the pills, there's something else beneath all of this, go discover that.'

And there's not a day that goes by that I don't thank my younger self for listening to that voice. There was a deep knowing within me that understood that I would have gotten sicker and sicker if I had continued down the path I was going on. I'd not have got to the root of my symptoms but rather just patched them up with pharmaceutical drugs and pushed down the associated emotions.

In amongst the ill health I'd been experiencing for those few years, I was also very much going through the motions of life. Rushing, *busyfying* myself, filling up my calendar weeks in advance, drinking bottles of wine in the week to calm my nerves, getting drunk after work every Friday only to feel terrible on Saturday—hungover and guilty that I'd done this to myself once again. I'd then spend Sunday worrying about the week ahead or going on a shopping binge in a desperate attempt to fill up the emptiness inside, only to keep repeating the pattern month after month, year after year.

And these strategies worked for short periods, but then the same feelings of emptiness would return. The thoughts that plagued my mind on repeat were, 'I'm bored. I'm too busy. I'm tired. I'm stressed'. And then this other thought would pop up and say, 'surely there must be more to life than this?'

Truthfully, I didn't know who I was anymore. I didn't know what I wanted in life, only what I didn't want. I knew I didn't want more of the same. I didn't want all of the trappings that come from buying a bigger house, a better car...that would keep me in a reality that had me feeling stuck.

I'd spent so many years trying to mould myself into the person that people wanted me to be—taking on all the feedback from parents, teachers, friends, co-workers, bosses over many years. And it had me spinning in confusion. 'Who the hell was I?' Surely my reason for being wasn't to live a life of other people's choosing. Surely my existence wasn't purely to make other people happy. But I was so addicted to proving my self worth by working hard that I didn't know how to get out of the mess I'd created.

Something was calling me deeper. But I had no idea what that was or where to find it.

Then one day, I was sitting at my desk at work, feeling those familiar empty feelings, mixed with tiredness, boredom and stress about how I would get all my work done. I looked out of the window and began zoning out into the distance—a familiar strategy to help numb out the pain. On this day, though, something incredible happened. It was as though a giant hand slapped me across the face. It woke me up out of my trance. There was a moment of clarity. The message I received said, 'what are you doing with your life?' 'You don't believe in what you're doing' You wouldn't even eat or drink the food that you're marketing', 'you're so misaligned with who you are'. It was a kick in the teeth. I knew that this was the truth I was avoiding. This was my higher self talking, waking me up out of the dream I'd been in.

And finally, I was ready to listen and do something about it.

I chose to repeat a familiar pattern that I'd used much of my life to get out of tricky situations. Run away. Run away from the discomfort and the pain. Thankfully, though, this time, the running away was also tied up with a dream and connected to my values of adventure, fun and curiosity.

Roll on another six months, and my partner and I were boarding a plane to Argentina from Melbourne, Australia, full of excitement and anticipation. We'd sold most of our belongings, had two very full backpacks, some money and a spirit for adventure. I was ready to finally explore my inner world and my heart as much as the outer world. I stepped into the trip with an intention to 'know me' and to reconnect with a sense of passion and purpose.

I distinctly remember that all of the physical symptoms disappeared when I stepped off that plane. Vertigo, skin rashes, nausea, headaches...they all went. And I've not had them since. It was a profound realisation to experience the real connection between the mind, the body and the soul firsthand. I recognised that my soul had been trying to communicate with me all along, but with a busy and resistant mind, the messages were only received fully once my body began to communicate via illness and disease, and I couldn't ignore them any longer. That's the thing with the body. It forces us to pay attention to what we've been ignoring.

But of course, this is not the end of the story. I had many years of emotions and memories to work through, years of putting up my defences and protecting my heart, years of accumulated stress held in my body in my rounded spine. And on every 15-hour bus journey as we travelled through windy valleys and endless straight highways, I looked out of the window at the Andes, at vast expanses of land, snow-capped mountains, llamas grazing, and the tears began to flow. Memories began to rise up—regrets, unresolved relationships, previous disagreements, moments of dishonouring myself and others, controlling behaviours, combined with dreams, desires and excitement for life. In these expansive lands, I was able to connect to an expansion in my body and mind. I could see more clearly. It was as though the heavy clouds were starting to lift. I was less caught in the stories and more able to see a greater perspective.

After about four months of travelling, my partner and I took a hike in Chile. While we scrambled through ice and snow to reach the peak of a mountain, I received what only can be described as 'downloads' or intuitive messages from my higher self—from spirit or guides...I don't know. What I did know was that this information felt more real than the life I'd been living for the past fifteen years. I was able to understand how sitting all day in a toxic work environment with artificial light, air, and ways of interacting was a deeply unhealthy existence.

I was able to see that now was a time for women to be in collaboration with one another and no longer in competition. I saw that my life mattered and that I could use my life for good in the world, knowing I had privileges that so many people in the world didn't have and that it was my responsibility to serve and speak up for those who couldn't.

The trip was a time to shed and to discover.

After eighteen months and 1000's of kilometres travelled, we flew to London from New York, ready to begin a new life in the UK. And while I felt more 'me' than I had in a long time, after such an epic adventure, I automatically fell into the same type of work that I was doing in Australia. And quite quickly, those same feelings began to arise. A boredom. A busyness. A knowing that there was more to life than this. That there was more for me to do in my lifetime.

It was frustrating, feeling like I was regressing, and a feeling of dread that I may become sick again. But something was different this time. I'd changed within myself. I wasn't going to go back there. I had a choice, and I knew that it was my responsibility to craft another more meaningful life for myself. I was also starting to show up differently at work. I was standing up for myself. I was speaking up in meetings more and refusing to work on unethical projects. I was finding my inner support and cheerleader.

But then I woke up one morning and couldn't get out of bed. My lower back had completely seized up. I was in agony. It was yet another wake-up call from my body to make some changes. I'd been commuting from London to the south of England for a few hours each day, for many months. Working on the train. Stressed with bad posture as I worked through an inbox of emails at 7:30 am.

When I eventually made it to a chiropractor, she asked if I did yoga. She asked me to do some yogic breaths as she manipulated my body. It was like magic. My back felt almost normal after just thirty minutes of treatment. From that point, I committed to undertake a regular yoga practice and study. It had always made me feel better in both body and mind, but I had just dabbled with it for years

Then one morning many months later, as I sat in another unfulfilling job, I had a flash of insight. I thought, perhaps my partner would honeymoon in India after our planned Thai wedding and then I could do my first yoga teacher training. My partner Tom had his usual look of surprise and resistance on his face when I proposed this, as yet again I crafted another plan of adventure and escape.

So, in 2014, we married in Thailand, honeymooned in Kerala and then parted ways for the next five weeks. I hadn't realised at that time what a profoundly life-changing experience this trip would be and how this was the point that would change my life and the way I saw it forever. This was the trip that brought me to my knees and brought me to my deepest, most authentic aspect of self.

It was a gruelling experience to undertake a 200-hour yoga teacher training in Ashtanga in Rishikesh. With the strange noises, constant traffic, 4 am starts, hours of practice and study and the constant thoughts that I wasn't good enough; flexible enough; knowledgeable enough. But despite all of this mind chatter, I was doing it. Showing up to chant and flow for two hours every morning.

Until I got sick. Really sick. Sicker than I'd ever been in my entire life. I could hardly get out of bed to visit the toilet. I was losing all of my fluids rapidly. After three days of delirious sleep, I was woken out of the delirium and mental fog once more by a loud internal voice that said, 'get out of bed now; you'll die if you don't'. Before I could understand what was happening, my body was out of bed, putting on my trousers that hung off my bony body. A moto driver drove me to the nearest hospital, an ashram with three beds. With rubble in the doorway, monkeys on the roof, flies buzzing around the dried blood on the beds and cows poking their heads into the ward, I felt a wave of absolute terror flood over me.

I wanted to run away again. This was the strategy that had worked all my life. But there I was, sicker than I'd ever been and confronted with one of my biggest fears: hospitals.

Hospitals have given me a feeling of dread and chills since childhood.

When the doctor spotted me, he took my pulse, looked at my tongue and, with a panicked look across his face, demanded that I be put on a drip immediately. I was severely dehydrated, and he was worried my kidneys may pack up soon. So, there I was, in India, on my own, with no option to run away from my fear. I had to face it head-on. And this was where things got real for me.

I remember being in and out of consciousness. There were five or six nurses around me, stabbing my arms to find a vein in my puny wrinkled arms. They were rushing around me in an anxious state as I felt utter terror running through my whole body. But I couldn't escape it. I couldn't run from it. I had to feel it fully. I felt the emotion move through me, only to find another familiar emotion appear: separateness, self-pity for being alone, 'why me' stories popping up. But then something else happened. These emotions passed, and suddenly I felt a wave of gratitude come over me—gratitude for being treated and cared for. I felt held and comforted by a greater force. I felt connected to everyone and everything. I felt peace and acceptance for myself and the situation I was in. I distinctly remember surrendering in that moment, 'if I am to die here, then I am ok with this'. I had let go of the resistance, the internal fight to the situation I was in. And I had a profound realisation and connection to my soul, my true authentic self.

In that moment, I realised that 'she', my soul, was with me all along. She wasn't to be found out there. She wasn't found in the job. She wasn't found in the bottles of wine. She wasn't found in the clothes shopping. She wasn't found in the trips overseas. She wasn't found in running away from discomfort. She was only discovered when I confronted and experienced my inner demons. My chronic need to run from pain and discomfort had been keeping me from her. I didn't need to prove anything to anyone. All I needed to do was to fully accept myself.

And I am forever thankful for India and for yoga for teaching me this and opening my heart and mind. If it wasn't for the asana, the breathwork, the meditation and the self-enquiry, I'm not sure I would have had this deep experience. My mind, body and spirit were primed for this breakthrough and transformation.

From that point, I knew that a big part of my calling and passion was to be a teacher and a guide, to support other people to reconnect with themselves. To have the tools and the know-how to heal themselves and know themselves on a deeper level. To become more self-empowered and connected to their intuition. And in turn, to connect to deeper fulfilment and purpose in their lives.

So fast forward through more adventures of living in different countries, more yoga and coaching studies.

And today I live with my husband back in Melbourne.

My husband is now living his dream of being a full-time artist.

And I'm healthier than I've been for most of my life. I have a great relationship with my inner world. I know how to meet and nourish myself; I know how to enquire and hold the parts of me that hurt; I know how to always follow intuitive impulses.

I uncaged myself. I broke free from my own limitations and stories, busted through my biggest fears and stayed true to myself, my passions and my calling in the process, despite how this was received by friends, family and society. I realised that the only approval I needed was from my own heart and soul.

For the past five years, I've been working with clients from all over the world, supporting them to overcome patterns of people-pleasing and burnout and to awaken their passion and aliveness so that they can live into the fulfilling and purposeful life that's calling them.

I deeply know that to honour yourself, your needs and your calling is one of the most generous and kind things you can do for yourself and the world.

Just imagine what the world would like if we all lived this way?

I choose to shine the torch for other people to do the same. To inspire and support others as they are awakening to themselves and to the possibility of their life.

As Maya Angelou so beautifully put it, 'Nothing can dim the light that shines from within'.

ABOUT THE AUTHOR
CLAIRE BRADSHAW

Claire Bradshaw is a certified holistic life and mindset coach, yoga teacher and host of the Becoming Whole podcast. She supports women worldwide, both privately and in powerful group containers, to be the leader of their own life—in business and in their relationships. Claire guides her clients to break free from automatic living and burn-out and to step into the passionate and powerful life that's truly calling them. She uses a unique blend of ancient yogic wisdom, proven coaching models and powerful questioning techniques to help her clients connect deeply with themselves, get out of their own way and bring their gifts out into the world. Her work is grounded in the belief that the world needs more of us to reclaim our authentic power, purpose and passion and express this for ourselves and for the future of humanity.

Website: www.claire-bradshaw.com
Instagram: https://www.instagram.com/_clairebradshaw_
Podcast: https://podcasts.apple.com/au/podcast/becoming-whole-podcast/id1267209074
Facebook: https://www.facebook.com/clairelouisebradshaw

DENISE MARSHALL

DARE TO LOOK WITHIN, SET YOURSELF FREE

I'm writing this chapter because I don't want you to have to suffer like I did. Maybe you can relate to some of my experiences, and maybe you can't. Regardless, I know that this chapter will touch those who are meant to hear it, and that is why I share my story.

I've always been a highly sensitive person. I feel everything so incredibly deep and can read my surroundings with x-ray vision. If I'm not careful, I start to absorb whatever is going on around me. Sometimes I will feel anxious or overwhelmed, and then a catastrophic event happens soon after. Or, I will be around someone with neck pain, and all of a sudden my neck starts hurting. I've had to learn ways to manage and protect my energy in order to function in the world. For all of my highly sensitive souls out there, I know how difficult it can be to get into your own energy when the external world is so loud. I also know what a gift it is to be a super feeler and knower—which lies within us all.

Knowing I wanted to make a positive difference in the world, I studied Adult Development at the University of Guelph and completed my Master of Social Work at the University of Toronto.

After completing my schooling and getting laid off from my job, I took time to decide what was best for me as I knew I hadn't been happy for a while. I had lost my childhood spark and was desperate to get it back. I ended up travelling to Thailand with my sister, and this is where I experienced a massive breakthrough in my personal development and spiritual journey. I started crying hysterically in a floating bungalow in Khao Sok and realized how disconnected from myself I had truly been. I decided that it was time to leave the long-term relationship I had been in for the previous five years and start to deeply heal myself and become the person I knew deep down I was meant to be.

I felt terribly broken at this point in my life. I had experienced several traumas that I was not able to adequately deal with despite attempts at seeking support. These traumas were paralyzing my ability to connect with my intuition and make empowered decisions. I didn't feel in control of my own life, and I constantly looked for answers outside of me. I frequently turned to substances to numb my pain and escape, when I knew this was only masking the truth of how deeply hurt and afraid I was. I had struggled with disordered eating and anorexia/bulimia-like tendencies, starting in university and never felt like I was enough. I wanted to reclaim control of life and my body. I was eager to be the bubbly kid that was happy to be alive and express herself freely once again. I wanted to feel freedom instead of entrapment.

Growing up, I developed some sort of inherent unworthiness about myself. This led to becoming extremely self-conscious and constantly comparing myself to others. It must have been a combination of society and the media constantly telling teens/young adolescents that they aren't good enough and setting unrealistic expectations regarding one's appearance and weight. For a good portion of my life, I felt like if I wasn't "perfect", I wasn't good enough. I thought that perfection actually existed and was attainable. Knowing what I know now, it's very clear why I felt chronically unhappy and never felt good enough for most of my life.

Through my own experiences, education and professional work, I know first-hand that trauma is the gateway for long standing addictions and emotional issues. I know the severe effects unhealed trauma has on one's development and self-esteem, ability to feel safe in the world and trust other people, be open to love, and make healthy decisions.

My parents got divorced when I was fifteen. I didn't see it coming and it totally shook up my entire world. Looking back, it makes you reflect on your childhood in a different way. It's kind of like grief that never really ends. As a kid, your family is everything, and having that dynamic volcano right in front of your face, well, kind of makes everything you've known feel like a big lie. As I've changed and evolved, I still feel this loss, especially as a super feeler. I've also learned that things just suck sometimes and you have to accept them and move on. Life isn't a Disney movie. In saying that, I am eternally grateful for family and friends who support me in my life, and who I know always have my back. Love always remains.

I've learned that as kids, we can often subconsciously blame ourselves for a lot of what happens or a lot of what our parents experience. We can somehow start to feel like it's our fault when mom gets angry when she misses the exit, or when dad gets fired from his job. Naturally, empathic and sensitive children want to save their parents and take away their pains. This is true for anyone in pain; there is an innate wanting to help. However, over the past few years I've learned that everyone is responsible for doing their own healing work and the only person you can change (because no one really needs saving) is yourself. I've learned that radical acceptance, forgiveness and compassion are key secret ingredients to healing, feeling empowered, and living a conscious, fulfilling, and meaningful life.

In high school, I loved academics and partying. Looking back, I have also learned that teenagers and alcohol is typically a recipe for disaster—at least it was in my experience. I have a few major scars that have been imprinted on my brain—nights I certainly wish I could take back—one's where I experienced sexual assault and rape. It's taken me years to be able to say this out loud, for the longest time I felt ashamed, as if it was somehow my fault. I know first-hand that trauma changes you and can morph you into a different version of yourself without adequate connection, healing, and support. However, I also know that every experience leads us where we are meant to be, and now I can help individuals heal from their own traumas and wounds, which is the thing I love doing the most. Call me an alchemist. (*chuckles*)

University was a lot more of me living out my trauma responses, drinking too much, and not caring about my well-being as much as I probably should have. In my mind, I was a smart-ish student, but not smart enough. I was skinny-ish, but not skinny enough. My mind was like a bully on the playground. I was doing "okay", but never felt enough. I felt a chronic emptiness and yearned for a deep feeling of love, connection, and true understanding. I sought out counselling at the health clinic on campus, but I didn't find much relief. I was frequently sick and exhausted. I dealt with various chronic conditions; the doctor's office had become a familiar place. Truthfully, it makes me cringe that I even have to share these details, but I feel it's important to address the depths of the mind and what it can become and the effects it has on the physical body as well.

At this point I also got into my first serious long-term relationship, which lasted for five to six years.

Looking back, the years after university, when I completed my Master of Social Work, were the most difficult. I became extremely disconnected from who I was. I knew I had to leave my relationship and heal myself, but was scared shitless of being on my own. I felt stuck in my current circumstances and didn't feel ready to take the leap. My soul craved freedom. My body became sicker. Self-sabotaging tendencies increased. I knew I needed to get back to the person I was before all of the shit that dulled my shine happened. I wanted to feel like my vibrant spunky self again. I wanted to be the girl who sang loudly and shamelessly in the car even when she didn't know the words, and the girl who loved being centre stage during her dance recitals as a kid. The person who didn't care what anyone thought and wasn't afraid to be seen and stand out.

Meanwhile, I was living in a condo in Toronto, not truly feeling a connection to my relationship, my job, or to myself. I felt more lost and less me with each day that passed. Life felt very hard, and I didn't even feel like I could truly enjoy it. I stopped doing activities that I loved at one point; I was putting my own needs last. I often found it difficult to enjoy life and "let loose". I was chronically worried, upset, and feeling not good enough. I was out of alignment with who I actually was, and was deeply being called back home. I forgot what a gift it was to truly be alive and experience the presence and beauty of life itself, despite the hardships that are ultimately part of the greater plan.

I was also experiencing that feeling in society that we are always taught to want more, that enough is never enough. I had started to get into holistic healing, but wasn't entirely sure what I was doing as looking inside for the answers was new to me. I had always found peace of mind on my yoga mat, but as I said, I felt like I completely gave up my life to make others happy. I was putting on a strong face, living for others instead of myself, and it was all crumbling away faster than I would've liked to admit. Denise was totally gone, and what she was chasing—a false version of perfection—didn't even exist.

The doctors prescribed medications to help me cope with my lack of motivation, inability to focus and the strong waves of emotions I experienced most of my life. After over a couple years of trial and error, I was frustrated with the number of medications I had been taking with massive side effects and little relief. I often cried, or had anger outbursts. I lost my period due to being such a low weight as the medication dramatically reduced my appetite. I truly felt broken and knew I wasn't being the person I was meant to be, despite reaching out for help through the mental health system and speaking with counsellors since I was fifteen, after my parent's divorce. I wasn't ashamed of asking for help; just nothing seemed to be working. It was time for me to go and discover who I was in the world as Denise. Not Denise with the trauma, or Denise with the boyfriend, just Denise. This is really where the journey began.

I came back from Thailand in November 2017, left my relationship and the condo where we were living together, and moved in with my sister. I started working with healers and coaches, and started a daily meditation practice. I began to enjoy my own company again, started remembering who I was and devoted the majority of my time to my spiritual practices and strengthening my connection to self and my inner child. I was ready to take control of my life and my decisions, instead of constantly seeking answers outside of myself.

I ended up getting a job in the geriatric field and quickly realized that a full-time office job was not conducive to my healing or mental health at the time. I felt trapped, like I had felt trapped in my relationship and previous condo living. Once again, my soul yearned for a sense of freedom. During this time, I had also started expressing myself online and sharing my self-healing journey. I wanted people to know that it is safe to express their true feelings and to share their stories. I was passionate about reducing the stigma of mental health and the reality of living with various diagnoses after trauma. I didn't want other people to suffer in silence like I had all those years of pretending I was okay and not finding adequate support through the mental health system, counselling, and medications. Suffering happens more intensely when we are isolated, connection is the magic ingredient. That is ultimately why I do what I do and what gets me up in the morning.

About a year later I was hit with a massive intuitive download to quit my job and start helping people online through my healing work. It was my "soul calling", and I had to listen. The feeling was overwhelming and I listened.

By this point I had gained ample experience interviewing and assessing others through my social work-related jobs and opportunities and abundance of self-learning that kept my light shining. I loved connecting deeply with individuals about the stuff that really matters, the tough stuff that keeps us stuck and afraid to make a move. The stuff that keeps us sad and down. The paralyzing dark fear that keeps you up at night. My gift is to help you light that shit up! I know how scary it can be to live in agony and fear, and I also know the relief and joy that is birthed when you take a massive leap of faith and choose your own happiness in a world that profits off keeping you co-dependent and feeling weak (*harsh truth*).

Quitting my job and leaving my relationship showed me two things.

First, my ability to believe in myself was a reminder that my life was in my hands and if I didn't like something, I could easily change it. I chose to become an empowered creator of my own life, trust my intuition, and ignore the doubts and insecurities telling me I wasn't good enough or that I was crazy for choosing an unconventional path. I refused to re-create a life of inner suffering and misery.

Second, it was a reminder that I didn't need to follow a traditional route of what society deems success. I didn't have to settle down, get married, and work a regular job before I turned thirty years old if it didn't feel right to me. I didn't have to sacrifice my happiness to keep someone else happy or self-sabotage my heart's desires to be accepted and or try to fit in. I allowed myself to be led by a greater power. I craved something deeper in life, and I am continuing to follow it. I decided to take time to unravel and recreate myself, without all the masking of deep insecurities and shadows. I chose to unlearn and begin again to create my desired reality.

Over the past three years, I've worked with multiple coaches to help me find my voice and show up online. My journey of entrepreneurship has been a roller coaster of self-discovery, self-love, self-trust, personal development, shadow work, inner child healing, and a whole lot of self-compassion and self-forgiveness (secret ingredients). It's also been one of the most spiritual awakening experiences I've ever endured. I found my sense of purpose, meaning, and belonging, which is what I was desperately seeking all these years. It was within me all along, and my heart finally cracked open.

I continue to do the work daily to rewire my subconscious programming and create new narratives in my life through self-healing, spiritual connection, meditation, yoga, and mindfulness techniques. I've learned that it is absolutely okay and sometimes necessary to take time to slow down and create the life you desire. It is never too late to start again. Always put your mental and emotional health first. Don't let the internet, family members, friends, or society rush you. You are in control of your life and you know what is best for you. This is what has been revealed to me through all of my experiences, hardships, and leaps of faith. There's truly been so much to share and integrate, and I continue to express myself online and guide other people to their own power and truth as well.

I'm not sure if I would have ever set my soul free if I didn't go to Thailand. If I didn't quit my job and start coaching, I would have never stepped into this deeper, more connected part of myself and be able to guide other individuals along their own healing path to inner strength and freedom as well. The healing journey is not an easy one; it is why a lot of people avoid looking at their trauma and continue to repeat cycles of intergenerational trauma, pain, and addictions. I have been deeply drawn to ancestral healing to continue to release, integrate and carve out a new way of being in the world.

I want this story to comfort you with knowing that even if you believe your trauma wasn't "that bad" or "could be worse", it doesn't need to be. Your experiences and feelings are valid, and I'm sorry if someone ever made you feel otherwise. You are allowed to be upset when things don't turn out how you planned. It is also safe to learn to re-trust and re-stabilize after traumatic experiences and choose to see the world through the lens of love, rather than fear. It is possible to uncover the truth of who you really are, without your wounding masking your light. It is possible to embody the fullest most vibrant version of you. It's possible to create your dreams and reach your goals, but remember, if you aren't in a place of inner peace with yourself, it still won't really feel that good when you get there. It's possible to start again.

ABOUT THE AUTHOR
DENISE MARSHALL

Denise is the founder of Finding Solid Ground, an intuitive life coach, self-healer, and empowerment guide. Denise studied her Master's of Social Work from the University of Toronto and currently runs a transformation healing community and works 1:1 with clients. Her work supports ambitious heart-centred individuals to step into their power by shifting into alignment with who they really are. Denise is trauma-informed and has helped many clients heal from past relationships and live life on purpose to manifest their dreams!

Denise considers herself a free thinker who is passionate about following her unique heart-led path in life where she believes the depths of joy and ease are found. Denise is currently focused on finding balance within her personal spiritual evolution, spending time on her yoga mat and drinking really strong coffee.

Business name: Finding Solid Ground
Instagram: https://www.instagram.com/denisejaclyn/?hl=en
Facebook: https://www.facebook.com/FindingSolidGround
LinkedIn: https://www.linkedin.com/in/findingsolidground

HOLLY LO

THE MESSAGE IN THE MESS

I remember the smell of the pine trees. The crisp cold air on my face. The quiet swish of skis through the snow. The gentle rocking motion of riding in the infant backpack carrier. My dad's occasional comment to me as he would point out a bunny in the trees or a bird. I was less than two years old, and I remember it so clearly, making it my earliest memory. I grew up with love and support around me, a typical 80s family in many ways, but with some special perks I have come to cherish. My mom was home with my sister and me when we were small, but she also pursued things she was good at, and I admired that. My dad was a local school teacher, much loved by his students. He taught me my love of the outdoors and sports. Faith played a huge role in my upbringing, not so much religion as a relationship with my Creator.

I realized as a young adult that I was an empath in the deepest sense of that term—taking on other people's emotions and energy. I would worry myself sick over problems that weren't mine. I became very good at rescuing others. I avoided conflict and mediated peace whenever I could in situations around me because that protected me from feeling their pain. It became so that I unintentionally built walls around my emotions to keep them safe and protected, or so I thought.

After a few serious relationships, I fell in love with my wild child husband: earrings, tattoos, and motorcycles! The match might've seemed unlikely to many who knew us, but the chemistry was real. So was the conflict. You couldn't find two more opposite souls in every way. After years of battling each other, I didn't know if I could keep going, keep facing another day and another set of challenges. Those walls grew stronger and higher around my heart, pushing him further out and folding in on myself. In the midst of this, I was facing stress-related health issues. We were told it would affect my ability to have children, but miraculously, our son surprised us out of nowhere. I firmly believe that life happens for you, not to you, and this was one such defining moment for me. After a traumatic birth in an ambulance, I struggled with PTSD for over a year without realizing it. The strain was almost unbearable some days. My mom and dad remained my rock through all the ups and downs we faced, and my husband had someone special in my dad as a friend and mentor. We were doing our best to hold our little family together but it was exhausting.

In the midst of it all, I had a deep, nagging feeling that there must be more to my life and abilities than just making it through each day. How many of you can relate? I see you mamas; you are hoping no one notices the pain you stuff down so you can care for the little ones that depend on you. You are praying for that miracle—finances, peace, health—hoping you can find the energy to keep trying. Maybe you are facing an uncertain future because things didn't go as planned. This feeling, this knowledge that I was capable of more, would whisper at me constantly, but the messy bits of my everyday life were louder. My child with high anxiety, my failing marriage, my tiny home daycare paycheque, and the stress of trying to block out everyone's negative energy left me with what felt like a complete mess. I would answer that whisper with "How?!" How could I possibly be something more?

On a misty May afternoon, after fighting for two hours to get my son to take a nap, he suddenly laid down and went to sleep. Across town, at the same time, my best friend laid down on the sofa to take a nap, and he never woke up. My whole world splintered that day. The mess no longer mattered. My dad was gone, in one breath, with no warning. I can't put into words how that felt in the moments and days following, but even now, twelve years later, the tears course down. I remember pulling up at the drive-through for a coffee order in the days that followed, and the woman cheerily asked me how my day was going. I went to say "fine" but instead, I broke down crying. And suddenly, that feeling rose up again. I am a mess. I thought things were bad before, now I am simply broken. That belief rooted deep and clung to the narrative I fed myself, that I had nothing left to give. The most amazing man just left this earth and yet the world had the nerve to keep turning. I had to keep getting up each day, love on my baby boy, and move forward somehow.

As the shock slowly dimmed, something interesting happened. That whisper that told me I was created for more started to get louder. In my brokenness, my mess, I was warring with the mindset that I really didn't matter and it wasn't worth the effort. I had dreams of my dad in the weeks following his death, where he would be calm and peaceful like he was in life, telling me I would be ok. I would wake from those dreams feeling so loved, forgetting for a second that he was gone and I was a wreck. From the outside, we had it all together. We were a very visible family with our businesses, and it felt like everyone looked up to us as this ideal. Very few ever experienced the mess. I realized I saw others the same way; the perfect Instagram feed, the Facebook videos of perfect homes and families, super successful women. It never felt like I belonged in that club.

Why do we forget to show the mess in the middle? No one is an overnight success, not in the real true sense of the word. We often only see the finished result. But what about the middle? I recently read a quote from Jamie Kern Lima that said, "When you have a higher purpose you go through your nevers", and that is where I found myself. I never imagined living without my dad to cheer me on in life. I'd never run a business of my own or been taught how to do that. My little family never had peace because of our relationship issues. But I knew I had to do something different to keep me going. Reasons usually come first; the answers come second. I had a reason, and the answer grew out of what I was already doing. I took a leap, closed our daycare, and opened a birth studio on the main street in town as a doula. I had no experience in business, no connections in the retail world, but I was passionate about serving women and families through their birthing journey. This evolved and grew into a baby boutique. At the same time, my husband made a career jump and became very successful as a real estate agent. For a short time, it felt like we were finally rolling in the right direction. So when we found out we were expecting our second baby, I took it in a stride, excited to grow our family. Seeing my husband's success inspired me to keep growing my own business, but with that came the added stress of learning through mistakes. I didn't have the budget to hire advertising or staff. Whatever profit I made was rolled back into inventory, and I grew resentful of my husband's ease of success.

I remember one difficult morning: after shoveling a good two feet of snow on the walkway to my shop's front door, ten weeks pregnant and nauseous, I was unable to get the door open because it was frozen. I sat down on the step in the snow and cried. I would never allow myself the "why me?" mentality, but it felt impossible at that moment. Two weeks later, in the middle of a bout with strep throat, I started spotting. Spotting turned to bleeding. A quick phone call to my midwife confirmed what I was hoping against hope was not true. I curled up on the sofa, fevered, aching, and now cramping with contractions, and wanted to fall apart. But I couldn't. Those walls that protected me, the ones I had spent years crafting, may have worked to keep me distant from some of the pain, but they also didn't allow healing in either. Sometimes, falling apart is how we get to a place of healing and rebuilding. At the time, it simply felt like I had messed it up somehow. If I hadn't shoveled so much snow...if I had gotten more rest...if I had been under less stress. My amazing midwife reminded me that as much as we cannot stop the body from doing what it is determined to do, we cannot provoke it if all was healthy and well, to begin with. As a doula, I understood that. I was able to be grateful my body worked perfectly even in miscarrying. However, my sweet four-year-old son didn't have that level of understanding, but he knew his mama was hurting. He laid by my side and stroked my hair. He brought me water and asked many times if I was ok. Thankfully, my mom and my husband were also with me through it that whole evening, not sure how to help but being strong for me.

I think of it now and cry every time, still finding healing and relief through tears that came so many years later. After the trauma of my first birth and the guilt I carried over it, this felt like a slap in the face. I imagined it like a punishment for the mess I had seemingly created. It left me with a burning desire to get it right, just once even. When we got pregnant with my beautiful rainbow baby a few months later, I promised myself I would do better. My business was in full swing. I loved my escape to my sweet little baby shop six days a week, often with my son joining me. I felt needed and respected there, with such amazing customers and mamas that became longtime friends. It was my safe place amid turmoil. It also left no time or energy to actually deal with what was building up behind those walls, the flood of anger, regret, shame, and anxiety. I continued to shove those aside so I could just keep moving forward, until just after new years when my daughter was born—a redemptive birth in so many ways. Everything was going according to plan. She was perfect.

A few months in, however, my daughter began struggling to breathe. What started as simple colds turned into serious cases of pneumonia and bronchitis over and over again. Trips to the ER, liquid steroids, puffers, nebulizers, medications that never seemed to help. While trying to maintain my business, care for my babies, and maintain that mess-free image, I was losing my own health. It's amazing to me how I was able to convince my mind that I was ok, while my body screamed, "no, you are not!"

After finally getting some answers at Sick Kids Hospital, I was determined to help my now one-year-old get well. One of my closest friends showed up at my store one afternoon with a bottle of essential oil to help with breathing, and I laughed. I felt like I was in the midst of a battle with Goliath, and she was handing me a stone. The great thing about friends who know you well is that they know your mess and love you through it. She knew I was desperate and needed help, but she also knew I was a skeptic. After showing me how to use this little bottle of oil, I promised I would give it a try for her sake, just to be supportive. That evening we did our usual bedtime routine of meds, but before I did any of her inhalers, I rubbed one drop of the oil in the inside of the mask, away from her skin. She did her breaths, and we went to bed. I woke up with a start, the sun shining in, and had the panic every mama feels when their baby sleeps through the night for the first time: are they ok? For us, though, this was a real concern. I hadn't had a full night's sleep in over five years, and that last year involved me sleeping with my baby girl to help her breathe through the night when she would wake multiple times. This was different. My first thought was, I'm afraid to look over at her. What if she isn't breathing? But when I saw her chubby pink cheeks and long eyelashes on the pillow beside me, breathing quietly, a warm wave of relief washed over me. That moment launched me in a direction I could never have imagined possible.

Over the course of a year, I dove into learning everything I could about holistic health and the power of oils that we were growing to love more every day. We never had another trip to the ER, and over time, we learned how to heal up her little body. I finally had space to get well and understand what my body was trying to tell me—to respect that voice and slow down enough to take care of me too. The changes were enough to convince this skeptic that I could probably share this knowledge with other mamas and my customers in similar situations. I started offering freebie Fridays at my baby boutique. Anyone could come get free oil samples and a listening ear to help support them in their health and wellness. I ate up every training I could find, every research paper and historical usage to grow my intuitive abilities into this area of wellness.

Behind the scenes, life was still messy, and we wasted so much precious time in our marriage battling our differences.

The stress still felt insurmountable to me, and I knew we were spiralling downward but honestly couldn't find the desire or energy to stop it. It came to a breaking point when I was expecting our third miracle. With a push in the right direction from my husband, I reluctantly chose to close my business and pursue this new adventure with my beautiful friend and mentor. As I continued to share my passion for serving mamas and their families with their health and wellness, my husband supported me and shared with those he knew needed it. But we were miles apart otherwise. I was blessed with powerful and gracious women who came into my business and caught the same vision and passion, and we grew rapidly into one of the top teams in the industry, especially in Canada. Our teams began to branch out globally, and I became a Canadian founder before I even really knew what that meant. I was running off of a drive to prove I could do this. I could actually make this work and not mess it up. I was looking at the very real possibility of being a single mom, and I wanted to be able to provide if that was the case. I was going to turn life's lessons into the skills I needed to succeed. I thought then I would no longer feel like such a mess. I wish I could go back a few years to this point and tell myself it doesn't work like that. Success, a higher level of leadership, only highlights the cracks in your armour and shows you where growth needs to happen.

After years of building walls and pushing it all down, I burnt out. Mothering, marriage, business, it all started crumbling, and I couldn't put it back together on my own. I couldn't fix it. But we decided we wanted to. Genuinely chose to seek help and start healing. I stopped running at Mach 3 and started saying no to speaking engagements and projects that didn't feed my soul, just my ego. When I took the time to reconnect with that voice, the one that always believed in me, that never thought I was messing things up, I found my passion again for life. He retired at thirty-eight and fell in love all over again with our kids. Over a year of growth, healing, and just breathing, I was able to rise to a whole new place of accomplishment I had been dreaming of. It has little to do with success and everything to do with listening. Being true to who you are in the depths of your core, the values that formed you and the vision that guides you, that voice will speak if you let it.

   I can't undo the unpleasant memories we created through this journey, just like I can't erase the mess that was made. Much like the ski tracks or boot prints my dad would make for me in the deep snow so I wouldn't get stuck, this journey may have left its imprint, but it also showed me the way. We can wallow, up to our knees, stuck in the mess that may or may not belong to us. Or, we can take a minute to hear the message in the mess and point our boots in the direction we need to go. I can't promise it won't still be messy, but I can promise you will grow and rise.

ABOUT THE AUTHOR
HOLLY LO

Holly Lo is an author, speaker, and multi-faceted entrepreneur who has merged her training, experience, and passion into a successful career. She is a former early childhood educator, competitive figure skating coach, and doula who learned the joys of teaching and supporting others. With the help of her husband, Holly co-founded doTERRA Canada, one of the largest essential oils regulatory companies globally, after trying essential oils to remedy her daughter's chronic illness when medical professionals were unsuccessful. She combined her passion for helping mamas in pregnancy, birth, post-partum, and newborn support with her love of natural health options and oils, and Oil Babies Ltd was born. Now a global business, Holly travels with her family, working with their customers and doTERRA teams all over the world. She has written two [insert adjective (ex: bestselling) and/or genre (ex: self-help)] books and co-authored two leadership books. She runs a podcast called Momdaze and a mom and baby product line, along with an online baby boutique. She is a mama to an incredible thirteen-year-old son, a sweet and sassy nine-year-old daughter, a mischievous six-year-old son, and a turtle.

Instagram: http://www.instagram.com/oil_babies
Facebook: www.facebook.com/oilbabies
TikTok: www.tiktok.com/oilbabies
Website: www.oilbabies.com

JEANNIE LYNCH

ILA'S MOON

The Moon represents powerful feminine energy. It signifies wisdom, intuition, birth, death and spiritual connection. The moon can also indicate a time of uncertainty and illusion—a time to trust your intuition so you can see beyond what is in front of you—when nothing is as it seems. The eight phases of the moon are seen as symbols to guide you on your own personal growth and development.

*(Note: The Moon definition is based on the Universal Waite Tarot Deck)

Phase One: The New Moon - New Beginnings

My story of transition begins with the decision to conceive my daughter Ila Anne three months after my wedding in 1995. My then-husband and I knew we wanted to start a family as soon as we got married. On this particular night in August, we got ready for bed with one clear intention—to conceive a child.

We stayed up late that night, sharing intimate details of our past and our hopes and dreams for the future. We both noticed the magnificent full moon shining through our bedroom window and promised to never forget it.

On this night, I felt empowered to stop being a victim of the shame, hurt, guilt, abandonment, and unworthiness I had experienced in my past. I was excited to be co-creating with someone who felt the same way. I remember feeling as if this was a dream come true and a perfect opportunity to close Pandora's box for good...or so I thought.

Ila Ann was born forty weeks later, on our first wedding anniversary. Nine months later, I found myself in another transition as my marriage fell apart. The divorce cost more than our wedding and took longer than the duration of our marriage. It became clear that Ila chose us both to be her parents, but for completely different reasons. In 1998, I became a single mom with sole custody and shared visitation.

Phase Two: The Waxing Crescent - Setting Intentions

Eight years later, on January 20, 2005, I received a call from Ila's step-mom, Stefanie, while driving to work. She informed me that Ila and her grandmother had been in a car accident and I needed to get to the hospital as soon as possible. I quickly turned the car around and headed straight there. I could feel the fear arise within me as I tried to take control of my thoughts. There was an intense tug-of-war between dismay and hope taking place in my mind. I phoned my sister Karen and shared the news I had just received and asked her to meet me at the hospital for moral support.

We arrived at the hospital at the same time and entered the emergency room together. We were both greeted at the door by the hospital social worker. She instructed us to follow her to a small room where we could talk in private.

The social worker explained:

"Jean, your daughter was in a car accident on her way to school this morning with her grandmother. Ila's grandmother was pronounced dead at the scene. The EMTs reported that your daughter was non-responsive when they arrived but were able to get her heart beating again on the way to the hospital. Your daughter has unfortunately suffered blunt trauma to her head and I'm afraid we need to prepare you for the possibility of your daughter living. In a few minutes, we will take you to see your daughter."

At that moment, the tug-of-war ended abruptly. I kept hearing the social worker's statement on repeat in my head as we began to walk down the hall to my daughter's room.

"We need to prepare you for the possibility of your daughter living."

When I entered her room, the first thing I noticed was that she did not look as if she had been in a bad accident. There was only one small bruise over her left eye, and I remember feeling grateful for that. I leaned over to kiss her cheek when the hospital machines started making loud noises. The room quickly filled with emergency room staff and I was asked politely to stand back.

I turned toward my sister in complete horror and began repeating the same questions to her: "What are they doing, what are they doing, tell them to stop, tell them to stop, what are they doing?"

Karen placed both her hands on my shoulders as if she could shake me back into my body. "Jean, they are trying to save your daughter's life".

I replied, "You don't get it, she's already gone, she's not there, a mother knows".

In that moment, instead of leaning into the situation in front of me, I backed out of the room and walked away. I will never fully comprehend why that was my choice; I only knew that standing there and hopelessly watching was too much to bear. I got halfway down the hall when I felt a tremendous, increasing weight pushing me down from the top of my shoulders until I felt my legs slip out from underneath me when everything went dark.

I woke to the sound of my daughter's voice speaking to me.

"Mommy, wake up it's me; it's time to spin this into gold".

When I was able to pull myself together, I turned to my sister and asked her to find someone in the hospital to talk to about organ donation.

Later that day, the doctors pronounced my daughter clinically dead. Her father and I agreed to take her off life support and give her organs to those who needed them. This was, and will always be, the worst day of my life. I remember leaving the hospital that day disappointed that I was still breathing.

Ila was laid to rest the following week under another full moon. At her service, her father and I shared how Ila would ask us to tell her "the moon story". I love that we both shared the same version of the moon story and found great solace that Ila knew the full moon would always be a symbol of our love for her.

Phase Three: The First Quarter Moon - Take Action

The first few months after Ila's passing were a blur. I will never forget the many acts of kindness and support we received from Ila's school, the local community, my employer, close friends and my family.

Going through this grieving process has taught me that some experiences seem so mundane and insignificant at the time, while others stay ingrained in your mind forever. This is especially true when you go through a traumatic experience. I've learned that every moment with my daughter mattered. Ila's passing has taught me to appreciate all of life's experiences as the gift they are, good or bad.

I'm going to share with you two of these notable moments and the three life lessons these experiences taught me. Coincidently, they both took place two weeks before and after Ila's passing.

Two weeks before Ila's passing, I went to my normal therapy session where I shared a particular worry with my counselor. I let him know that I had a strong **sense** that the time with my daughter was about to be cut short. I gave him a few other examples of when these kinds of thoughts would later play out and come true. I joked with him that I had a crystal ball and explained that many people had told me that this was some kind of "gift", but I knew differently. I believed the knowing was a **curse**.

He tried to comfort me that these thoughts and worries were completely normal. He suggested meditation or yoga to help ease my mind. He also suggested I pick up a few books on developing my Intuition.

Two weeks after Ila's passing, I went back to the same counselor. We talked for over an hour about the day Ila died. These were the first steps in processing my grief, and today I acknowledge they were the most important. I remember asking, "Now what?" at the end of the session.

His answer:

"Jeannie, there will come a day when you will realize that what you're here to do is to help others heal. It's time to embrace the gifts you have instead of being afraid of them. I would like to suggest that today is our last session. I would like to make a referral to a colleague of mine, I believe she can help you develop these gifts."

At the time, his answer made no sense to me. I was confused as to what gifts he was even talking about. The referral to another counselor would end up being my next steps on my healing journey. These experiences taught me these three lessons: 1) Everything in your life is happening for you, rather than happening to you." 2) Every experience, especially those involving other people, is significant 3) The best part of your life is when you embrace the magic and synchronicity of a mind-blowing coincidence.

Phase Four: The Waxing Gibbous - Refine & Home

I started working with my new counselor immediately. At this point, I was showing signs of post-traumatic stress syndrome and having involuntary out-of-body experiences. It was a blessing that my new counselor was also an energy healer, and many of our therapy sessions ended with me receiving an energy healing.

Six months after my daughter's passing, I was immersed in all things mystic. I was laser-focused on developing my own Intuition. I was learning to trust my divine guidance and trying to follow the path of least resistance. That path included meditation, the chakra system, yoga, Buddhism, mindfulness, the law of attraction, intuitive readings, mediumship, Reiki healings, past-lives exploration, and a deep-dive into this idea of an afterlife.

Finding and following a spiritual path has been one of the most rewarding adventures in my life. I've learned that an entirely new way of life will emerge once you're open to receiving divine guidance. I'd like to share one of these experiences that took place. It is the story of Ila's Moon. This story is for anyone who has lost a loved one and wants to believe that <u>Love Lives On</u>.

My neighbor invited me to a party that some of the parents from Ila's class would be attending. This would be my first attempt at a social gathering.

When I entered the party, I noticed the mother of one of my daughter's closest friends. I headed straight toward her and we wrapped our arms around each other in a heartfelt mother-to-mother hug. She told me that it felt like a coincidence to be seeing me just then. Just before the party, her daughter had written a poem and absolutely insisted that she hear it before leaving. She heard the poem and immediately thought of Ila. She promised she would email me the poem the next day.

As promised, the next day I received the following poem

If you are up at half past nine
When the moon is up in the star lit sky
You will know why the moon is there
To shine a bright glittery trail
To a place where happiness is all there is
No wars, no guns, no need to fight
That's the place I'll be tonight.
Poem By: Alyssa Tenney - age 8

I broke down with tears of joy as I read the poem. I felt it was a direct message from my daughter. I immediately responded to her email with a sincere "thank you" and shared the significance of the poem.

The next full moon would be just a few weeks away on August 9. I marked the date in my calendar, created an alert on my phone called "Ila's Moon", and went back to work with a feeling of contentment and connection to my daughter.

Phase Five: The Full Moon - Fruition and Completion

A few weeks later, I heard the alert go off on my phone. I was driving on the interstate, on my way home from work, when I began my intense search for

"Ila's Moon". When I took my last turn, I found the most magnificent moon I've ever seen—it had a shimmering halo around its circumference and seemed larger than I had ever noticed. I quickly pulled over to the side of the road, too overwhelmed to drive. I felt my daughter's energy enter the car, and I cried tears of joy. I knew she was right there with me, and I began to speak out loud to her.

"Yes, sweetie, I see. I <u>know</u>. I understand and I appreciate the message. I love you, too, Little I. Thank you so much."

When our time together felt complete, I pulled back on the road and checked the time. It was half-past nine. It was just as the poem said it would be! It was also ten years to the day and minute Ila was conceived.

Phase Six: The Waning Gibbous - Introspection

The full moon experience changed my understanding of how spirits could communicate with us. I knew I wanted to learn more about how to do this for the people I was coaching.

A few weeks later, a close friend of mine invited me to a four-day conference called "Life After Loss" at the Omega Institute in Rhinebeck, New York. Many of the presenters were authors of the spiritual books I had been reading—Dr. Brian L. Weiss, Sonia Choquette, Raymond Moody M.D, and John Holland, to name a few favorites.

On the last day of the conference, John Holland, a world-renowned medium, hosted an event that would allow the attendees the opportunity to connect with their loved ones in spirit. My daughter was the first spirit through. The message I received changed my life forever.

Ila's message through John Holland

"I have a message from a little girl who would like to make a connection to her mommy. She is showing me and telling me she wants her mom to know that she is 'The Line Leader'. I am seeing she is very young and her job in spirit is to line up the mothers that you will work with. They are like you, they are grieving. She is telling me that you will help them heal. Her name is I, or Lila, Eli... does this mean anything to anyone?

She is also telling me that the man standing next to you is not her daddy, that you and her daddy are no longer together. Does this mean anything to anyone who is standing over here?"

He pointed in my direction.

Sitting in a crowd with other grieving parents, I raised my hand and replied nervously, "I think that's me". His message went on to tell me so many important details about the day she passed—what it was like to transition and how she got there. He told me she knew I was grieving and asked If I was ready to let go of the pain. Ila wanted me to know that she loved her daddy and me and suggested that we come together in our **love** for her, not in our **grief**. He explained that our work together was not over. It had only just begun.

Phase Seven: The Last Quarter - Forgiveness

I came back from the conference clear-eyed and excited for my life with my daughter in this new way. I was finally able to embrace my intuition and wanted to teach others to do the same. I began doing spiritual readings to help other mothers connect with their loved ones. I did not want Ila's passing to define my entire life, but I was willing to let it be my gift to offer.

Phase Eight: The Waning Crescent - Surrender

Early in my spiritual journey, I believed that our life was merely "**God's School**" and that every experience was a predetermined life lesson. I thought life was only about lessons and that how we handled these teachable moments would depend on whether or not we needed to repeat the lesson.

My current understanding is considerably broader than that. I now believe that our life is our true **desire** to **feel** these experiences while we're in a physical body. Everyone collectively benefits from these shared experiences because we are all eternal and <u>ONE</u>. These experiences are the **sensations** of good and bad, joy and sadness, love and loss, relationships and betrayal, rest and hard work, the blessing of birth and the sweet transition back home.

Today, I live in Florida with the love of my life and our K9 Search & Rescue dog, Molly. Ila continues to be the "Line Leader" for the clients I serve. I'm happy to share that rather than grief, I feel a strong connection to my daughter's spirit. My heart is full of love and appreciation for every experience that comes my way.

...and so it is.
Love and appreciation,
Jeannie :)

ABOUT THE AUTHOR
JEANNIE LYNCH

Jeannie Lynch is an intuitive energy healer, spirit coach, teacher and content creator on YouTube. Jeannie's spiritual coaching business focuses on helping her clients navigate through difficult times by giving them the tools and resources to assist them along their healing journey. She works with her clients to identify and remove negative energy blocks, limiting beliefs, unhealthy thoughts or patterns that prevent them from living the life their **soul intended**.

After twenty-five years, Jeannie left her corporate job in finance to move to Florida, where she started her own coaching practice. After years of helping women business owners start and market their own businesses, she made the brave decision to do it for herself. Her desire is to **Change the World One Video/Podcast at A Time and help her clients be the best expression of themselves.**

YouTube: https://www.youtube.com/c/JeannieLynch
Podcast: https://podcasts.apple.com/us/podcast
Facebook: https://www.facebook.com/meanjean1963/?
Instagram: https://www.instagram.com/jelila63
LinkedIn: https://www.linkedin.com/in/jeannie-l
Twitter: https://twitter.com/Jelila63Lynch
Spotify: https://open.spotify.com/show/0HNPGnA
TikTok: https://vm.tiktok.com/ZMe45naG4
Email: jelila63@gmail.com

JENNIFER BERTONE

BIRTHING A GODDESS

I was thirty-seven weeks and four days pregnant with Azure, our second son. On August 16th, 2020, I woke up out of my sleep with contractions that shook my body with pain. I was unsure if this was the real deal because I had been having these contractions for two weeks straight. And for the fifth night in a row, I felt terrible for waking up Julio, my partner, to tell him this might be it. I rolled over slowly in between the hard contractions that began coming closer together and tapped Julio to let him know I thought this was it. My body automatically took a deep breath and then—wait a minute; this is it! These contractions felt heavier and more profound, and my mind connected with Azure's. He was ready.

I slowly moved to my yoga ball between contractions to get comfortable and time how far apart they were. It was around 1:30 am, and I was quickly assured by how close my contractions were that I needed to call my midwife and let her know *this is it*.

Julio began running hot water down the hose from our faucet and into the birthing tub we had blown up a few days prior. We positioned the birthing tub right in front of our bed so I could crawl back into bed with no problem when the baby came. This was my first home birth and my first water birthing experience, and I remember others saying laboring and birthing in the water was magical. I was looking forward to the moment I could step into the tub and float. I've always had a special connection with water. It's an element my soul desires and loves deeply. So birthing this baby in a space where I felt held and in peace was essential to me.

I quickly threw on a bathing suit and a white tank top over it while the tub was filling up. I wanted to be in something easy to remove and comfortable to be in. The tub was almost ready when our midwife arrived around 3 am.

She began setting up her equipment as I submerged my body into the warm water and began to dive within. I didn't know where my headspace should've been. I just knew I was trying my best to stay calm and relaxed for the sake of myself and Azure. At the same time, I was focused on not allowing the fears that were indoctrinated within me from the labor and birth of our first son, Kyngzly, from the hospital staff. All at once, my mind was nowhere and everywhere.

I had previously told Julio that I wanted to take photos and video of the labor and birth, so he quickly set up our camera and took some snapshots of me laboring. I'm so thankful for those photos. For 5 am, he was a pretty great cameraman.

I sat in that birthing tub for seven hours straight. Seven hours! I was a prune. But it felt good, so I listened to my body. This whole process, I felt, was a test to listen within and use my power to birth this baby. I tried my best to focus on just that.

My midwife suggested I step out of the tub and walk around to help Azure drop down and get into a good spot for him to come through. My contractions were so painful at his point, and I thought I was dying. The fears that flooded my brain from my last birth came in. The fears that others had shared with me while pregnant came in. For a few minutes, I cried. I let myself release that energy of fear. I repeated over and over again to Julio, " I don't know if I can do this," and "am I going to make it out of this?" Each time he assured me with words of affirmation and reminded me of my why. He also said something I'll never forget. He said, "the only way out is through." Those words gave me so much motivation and energy to push through and use what energy I did have to birth this baby.

I quickly managed to stand up in between contractions to get out of the tub. Julio held up my robe and wrapped it around me so we could walk outside together. Our bedroom sliding door leads out to the pool patio in our backyard. We walked only a few feet out of the house before I had to bend over and grab the side of our patio furniture. My midwife wasn't joking when she said walking would help speed things up.

At this point, my water still had not broken, but my midwife assured me that it was perfectly normal, but at the same time, it could be what's holding the baby up. This frustrated me. She told me I could potentially pinch my bag of water if I could reach it and break it myself. I tried her advice once I got back in the tub after wandering outside for a little while. I couldn't break my water. I felt even more defeated at this point, and I was so tired. I had never been this tired in my life.

It was getting close to noon, and my body began to take over. I couldn't believe the pain I was feeling. At one point, I remember trying to leave my body mentally. I tried so hard to put myself in deep meditation and zone out from it all. But I remembered what another wise and seasoned home birth mother had shared with me one time. She said, "Pain is power, and you must lean into the pain." This finally made sense. I realized every time I tried not to feel the pain of the contraction, my body closed up, which held the baby back from coming. I had to be present in every moment because every time I leaned into the pain, the baby moved down, and the pain grew stronger. But we were making progress. I was making progress.

I began crying again. My emotions were engulfing me like tidal waves as I was on my knees with my arms and head hung over the side of the tub, allowing gravity to do its thing. My body began to take over even more. My body pushed. I took a breath. My body pushed again. I took another quick breath. I was in disbelief of this process even though I was living it. It was like my body was a separate entity. Proof that our body has control, that our bodies have the power to do hard things even when our mind tells us differently.

Julio pushed down on my tailbone to help with the pressure I was feeling. This felt amazing.

I leaned into the pain some more. And some more. And then, I felt that "ring of fire." That burning sensation when the baby is coming through and stretching your tissues. My midwife gently guided me to slow down at this point and allow my body a moment to process. I tried to slow down the best I could, but you can't stop a baby from coming! My body continued pushing on its own. Each time was taking my breath away.

And then, Azure's head came through, and I felt my waters burst and release a ton of tension. I was so happy and scared all at once. It was go time. My midwife assured me I could take my time and push how I needed. I loved how she cared for me just as much as she cared for Azure. So often, mothers are neglected.

I heard words of love and encouragement from Julio, and his voice began to crack. He could see Azure. And I think he could see a new me. Our older son Kyngzly was hanging on Julio's back as he bent down next to the tub. This whole time Kyngzly was wandering around the room, playing games and enjoying snacks. He thought I was swimming all day!

All in the exact moment, Julio shuffled around the room to grab the camera. As he returned, Azure's body came through, and he floated gently into the warm water of the tub and into my shaky hands. I caught my own baby. I scooped him up and placed his head on my tired body. Holding his head full of dark brown hair, we laid chest to chest. Heart to heart. Encapsulated in our energy of love. Nothing outside of that room existed—just us. The pain from my body lifted instantly, and I was at peace. "I did it. I did it. We did it. It's over. It's over." I repeated out loud.

****

I don't come from a family of emotionally aware women. I don't come from a family where home birth is thought of as an option. I don't come from a family of women who are in tune with themselves. I don't come from a family that is body-positive. I don't come from a family with the desire and deep need to connect with their ancestors. But I am all of those things.

I come from an abusive home. I come from an emotionally volatile family. I come from a body-shaming father. I come from conditional love. I come from fear and guilt, and resentment. And yet, I am none of those things.

My father shamed me for breastfeeding my first child and made me feel disgusting. He made me feel like I was wrong. He made me uncomfortable and unsafe. Three months after giving birth to Azure, I tried to get my flow of loving my body back. I was mentally okay but still adjusting to having two young children and my body healing. I overheard my father say, "her stomach looks big and still pregnant," in a very judgmental tone. I wish I could say that it didn't bother me. I wish I could say that didn't crush me. But it did. I was the heaviest I had ever been, and hearing that said from an outsider made me feel gross. I didn't feel beautiful. I didn't feel good about myself at all. It felt like a little piece of how proud I was of myself, and my body for accomplishing a home birth was taken away. I felt broken. I have experienced copious amounts of situations just like these my whole life. Situations that made me feel powerless and experiences that disconnected me from my womb.

That same night I prayed. I prayed to stay on this path and to feel confident again. To continue to not let outside distractions steer me away from my knowing and truth.

In the following days, something began to change within me. I started doing the work that matched the energy of the liberation that came from my home birth. Having a home birth showed me my power in many ways. It showed me I could do hard things and reach new depths of my truth. It showed me that I get to determine how things in my life will go because I am in control. I began using that energy of sadness and grief and turning it into my power.

I have the amazing home birth story that I do and why I share it because I worked hard for that story. I fought and fought my way to happiness. I fought for my freedom. I consciously did the work. I showed up for myself. My whole life, I have been breaking free from toxic generational habits and programs. And this experience was no different. I rewrote the story of my womb and womb care by having a home birth, so all the women after me could know they could do the same. I paved a new path—one that was liberating and free and, most importantly, full of love.

I soon realized that those sad times of my family not accepting me, my family not believing in me and judging me, allowed me to live in my truth more than ever. Because if that pressure wasn't present, why would I have changed? I changed because the stress pushed me. I changed because, in moments of hurt, I chose myself. And that's how I found my path. Homebirth is how I found my way. Going through with something I knew was my truth, no matter how little support I had.

I applied this perspective to all areas and times in my life where I was hurt, abused, or emotionally unwell. I had profound healings while using this perspective to look at my life during those times. Honestly, the bottom line, if I didn't grow through those hard times, I wouldn't be where I am today. And I love where I am today, which brings so much gratitude and love for those hard times, flooding my heart with healings.

Immediately after my home birth experience, my life began changing. My soul was in the front seat, and I was listening. I'm one woman, but we are all connected. My hurt is your hurt. And your hurt is my hurt. If one of us is wounded, we all are. I felt my soul guide me in the direction of helping other mothers and women find their voice and power. I knew my story had to be heard. I knew my story could be what shows another woman that she does have the choice to have an amazing experience while pregnant, laboring, and postpartum. We deserve nothing less than that. We, as women, deserve that village of help. We deserve unconditional love and support through all seasons of life. We are the creators of this reality. We nurture, protect, provide and love. We deserve that in return.

Tapping into my womb wisdom allowed me to channel my ancestors more deeply. I aligned my life with ancestral healing methods: essential oils, teas, and other natural remedies. I am a healer. But not someone who waves her hand over your head, and your headache is gone. No. Although that would be kind of cool.

I am a healer that channels the wisdom from the women of my lineage. I channel the wisdom from my past lives and all of my angels that guide me. I help others step into their power by taking control of their health, mind, and soul. Whether through healing with essential oils, food, and other natural remedies or stepping into your power through home birth. Both callings I channel wisdom for, endlessly and with love.

Mother or not, you're powerful. And to be alive during this time, you are here for a reason. We all have our missions. No matter what that mission looks like, know this: the rules you feel you need to follow are just rules made up by someone who paved a new path. If they don't align with your truth, **pave your own way.**

ABOUT THE AUTHOR
JENNIFER BERTONE

Jennifer is a priestess, mother and creator who guides women on a journey within to take back and remember their power. She is the founder of Lemurian Design Co., The Oily Soul Temple, Birthing a Goddess, and The Lemurian Post Newsletter.

Jennifer provides home-birth mentorship, intentional artistry rooted in love and reminds everyone of their individual capacity to heal their own vessels intuitively through natural ancestral practices. A mother of two small children, she has already assisted many incredible women to break free of indoctrinations and limiting beliefs. Having a lifelong passion for art that embodies joy and love and a deep desire to help women find new levels of liberation, Jennifer creates, teaches and leads through one-on-one mentorship, group workshops and customized art.

Instagram: https://www.instagram.com/lifeofthe_enlightened
Email: birthingagoddess@gmail.com

JUDY LYNN MITCHELL

WHEN YOUR SOUL SPEAKS... LISTEN

As I lay on my bedroom floor in tears, I wondered, *is this what my life is going to be like? Is this all there is to life? Why am I experiencing this?* These were some of the many questions that floated around in my mind as I struggled to exist and as I cried myself to sleep many nights.

But, let's back up a bit...

I was taught the traditional societal plan ... that you should get good grades, go to college, get married, have kids, get a good-paying job, retire and die. Wow... Is that what my life is "supposed" to look like? Well, needless to say, I did not resonate with this.

To narrow the path further, I came from a lineage of heavy Catholicism, which was full of rules as to how your life should be—that you were to attend church every Sunday, you were taught what you should believe in, etc.and if you veered from this, you were a sinner. There was such guilt, shame and judgement that accompanied this. You felt like you weren't good enough, like you were a failure, like you were a disappointment, along with many other emotions and beliefs. In addition, there was the fear that you held over the concept that you would go to "hell" if you didn't follow the rules. Religion is a topic that is near and dear to my heart. I have overcome some of these beliefs and fears by asking questions, researching and trusting my intuition regarding God and all the "manmade" religions that exist. It's a whole other book that I could write about, and I may one day as I still have so many questions about its creation and the truth and availability of the scriptures that exist.

I grew up in a generation where kids should be seen and not heard. This was part of my foundation and veers its ugly head every time I attempt to be "seen" in the world today. My belief system was ancestral and created from all of my life experiences.

I began to question my belief system and asked, *what really happens if I don't follow the rules, beliefs and stories that I was taught and those that I created?* They felt so limiting, so structured and so draining. I also didn't understand why I felt my soul crying inside despite following the "rules"... I was NOT living, but rather only existing. I had such a longing for more, a desire to seek answers to all the questions that I had.

I was always able to sense things that others couldn't—just know things that I couldn't explain—and I started to have premonitions in dream form when I became pregnant with my daughter. I would dream or have visions of an event and then it would occur. I also had the gift of creating things that I wanted in life. I'd plan out what I wanted to experience, and it would show up. I never knew what all of this meant then, but I now see that this was the beginning of my clairs opening and my unique abilities starting to surface.

I ended up in a toxic marriage, but divorce was against my religion, so according to this, I was stuck. As time went on, things escalated, and I was losing the essence of who I was. During this time, my baba (grandma), who recently passed away, started to come to me in my dreams. These were more than dreams; they were messages from her. Her presence became very real. It was as if she walked along side me. Now, I know that she did. My fears became heightened and my ego stepped up; "where will you go, how will you support your daughter and you, what will others think, etc.". Through the voice of my baba, I found my strength within, knowing that I was going to be taken care of and acknowledged that it was ok to go. That we would be ok. And we were.

My baba's strong presence left me that day as I started to walk a new path. I moved forward, not acknowledging what I'd just been through, all of the emotional pain, the trauma of divorce and the new damaging beliefs that I created. I thought I was on my way to a new life when, BOOM, I had attracted the same toxic energy, the patterns of abuse and a similar type of a man. However, little did I know this would be way worse. The universe would make it clear this time (since I didn't get it the first time). This time it came in the form of lies, alcohol, cheating, drama and abuse... this was way beyond what I previously lived. What was happening to me? How did I attract this and on such a deeper level? Is my life just destined to be in turmoil? Will I ever find real love? Do I stay and live this life accepting that this is all I'm ever going to be and that this is just how life is... do I settle for this?"

My heart ached, knowing this didn't feel right.

What was life all about? My questions led to a deep yearning to seek out why we attract the people, situations and things that we do. There must be a way to stop it and I would not rest till I found these answers.

Once again, all the beliefs and fears started to surface to keep me there, "what will others think, you can't leave, look what happened last time, it's just going to be the same again...", but I didn't listen because I knew I deserved better,

I was worth more, and if I didn't quite fully believe it yet, I DID know that my daughter didn't deserve this environment. So we parted ways.

Two failed marriages behind me...now what?

I didn't love myself, I didn't truly respect myself, I didn't know my full worth, I didn't feel deserving of real love, nor did I believe that it even existed.

But this time was different as I had such a strong pull to figure all of this out because I was NOT going through this again.

So, I moved again. I started a new job as a supervisor with Alberta Health Services and carried on. I was as far up the corporate ladder as I had wanted to be in my career, yet how could a career that I thrived in all my life not feed my soul all of a sudden?

It was time that I acknowledged what I'd been through and to FEEL all those emotions. It was time to heal. I was drawn to alternative ways of healing and energy work. I couldn't read enough books and take enough courses to satiate my thirst for this knowledge. It fascinated me and explained so much as to why I had attracted the marriages, the people and the experiences in my life that I did. Finally, I was beginning to find the reason behind all of this trauma.

So, certification after certification, I began to see and feel that there was something more to all of this, something deeper. I became a Usui Reiki Master. I received my certificates in Rahanni, Thai hand/foot reflexology, colour/sound therapy and animal reiki. However, I was still being called to go "deeper". I was drawn to the Akashic Records and received my certification as an Akashic Records practitioner, and this became a huge turning point for me.

I left a career that served me well for twenty-five years to follow a "calling" that I had deep within. It was unexplainable. I never understood what the word "calling" meant until I experienced it firsthand. I then opened my own business, Holistic Modalities, with the intention to help others suffering through this as I was.

Little did I know that this step meant letting go of a label I placed on myself of who I was. It meant finally releasing the belief of "what will others think" and meant reframing a new belief of what success meant, how I defined security in the form of a guaranteed monthly paycheque, and so much more.

The struggles of setting up your own business, your online presence, marketing, etc. were all additional factors in this as well. It was all new to me, but at this point, I had no choice but to figure it all out. By this time, my ego was in full force, saying, "what did you do, look what you had, how are you going to support yourself and your daughter now, etc.".

Throughout all of this, I was still being called to go "deeper" and retrace my steps to as far back as I could remember of my traumas and pain. In doing this, I was channelled—a process in which I put in tangible form to teach others on this same journey. I created an eight-week mastermind to clear limiting beliefs, negative patterns and fears by using the sacred tool of the Akashic Records. The more healing work I did on myself and for others, the stronger my connection to a higher power became. I started to see energy and auras around people, animals and objects. I started to hear more messages. I saw more signs, i.e. coins, feathers, repetitive animals, numbers, flickering lights, etc., and I began to trust in ME. I never saw anything as a coincidence again, but rather as another area that I needed to explore, another breadcrumb on the trail to my highest self.

I acknowledged that I attracted everything I did in my life and that my deepest darkest moments were teaching me lessons that my soul needed to learn in order to grow. I was thankful for my journey because, without it, I would've never learned what I did, found my voice, realized my worth and recognized that it was my thought system that was keeping me stuck all along.

I created a path of communication to the spiritual world in which I would receive answers to questions, direction or just messages. I started to see symbols of what looked like DNA strands floating before me in a holographic manner. I knew this all meant something and began to seek out other spiritual leaders— that had already walked this path, for assistance. I would never have come this far without the guidance of others farther along this journey. This path is NOT to be walked alone. Everyone is on a different level of growth. I quickly learned that it's set out this way so that we don't have to struggle on our own so that we can reach out for guidance and be fast-tracked along our journeys with the assistance of someone that's already been there.

At this time, my gift of being able to manifest was heightened. I always had the ability to create things but never knew that's what I was actually doing. Instead, I was told I was just lucky.

I desired to teach this, but I received a message saying, "in order to teach this, you must first experience it". I thought I did, but now I know that I wasn't seeing the whole picture. Let me explain… the perfect opportunity for creation arrived in which we were looking to move to an acreage, so I thought, how about I consciously create our ideal acreage? So I began to create a wish list, all of the must-haves and our additional desires. I worked on manifesting this daily (sometimes even three times a day) for nearly six months, but I also had an additional request…that our current house was not to sell until our ideal acreage arrived. So I set this intention, and after six months of patiently waiting, watching showing after showing, our acreage came to fruition. The next day, we went to see the acreage and that same night after the thirty-fifth showing, we received an offer on our house and accepted it. It was a day of magic... but only because I BELIEVED I could create this.

There was a lot more to this process but for the sake of this chapter, you are reading the condensed version. After this amazing "exact" creation, it hit me... everything came together... while I was creating this, I was also working through my beliefs and fears along the way! There were a lot that surfaced, but the one belief and fear in particular (that was my "aha" moment) was that deep down, I didn't believe I was worthy or deserving of receiving this, and a fear of mine was that whenever I received something, it was always taken away. Therefore, how would this be any different? Well, it was different because I located the root cause of this belief and fear and was able to release it. When I did, everything fell into place. I co-created our dream with the universe. Wow, is this how powerful we are when nothing's standing in our way?

Yes, it is.

What I teach today is gathered from the path that I walked. You are NEVER stuck. Your thoughts are what create your reality. You attract the things you do in this lifetime to learn your soul lessons and grow. Your beliefs, fears, patterns and perceptions are what hold you back from being who you want to be. When you locate the root cause of these, learn your soul lessons, release them and expand your thought system, you become unstoppable! You also then have a deep understanding and sincere gratitude for the path you walked.

It truly is as simple as that.

When you believe in yourself, when you find your worth, when you love yourself, the possibilities become limitless for you. It's truly a beautiful revelation, and I am your "true story" that this is possible for each and every one of you.

You are such a powerful vessel that can consciously create whatever you wish to experience in this lifetime... you just must first believe that you can! This life is beautiful, this world is amazing, and you are extraordinarily powerful. It is your birthright to live in abundance if you so choose...it is truly a conscious choice.

My new program utilizes all of my gifts in being able to locate the root causes of your fears, limiting beliefs and patterns to clear these from your energetic system, to channel messages and healing for your highest regard and my manifestation process. In addition, I teach you how to access your own Akashic Records so that you can learn to do all of this on your own.

Your purpose in life is in your evolution and growth. Nothing that is meant for you to experience in this lifetime will ever pass you by. There is no "destination", but rather, it's all about the journey. Trust in the process and live your life with love and compassion for yourself and others.

My wish for you is to release all that is holding you back and keeping you stuck. This world is full of endless possibilities and opportunities for you to create a life of abundance. There is no rulebook in this lifetime, but rather a book of blank pages of which you are the author. So, create from a perspective of no limits, no boundaries, no right or wrong and no rules.

I leave you with this: if I knew then what I know now, what advice would I give to my younger self?

- The only thing that stops you from becoming everything you want to be is YOU!
- There are no mistakes in this lifetime, but only opportunities for growth, from your soul lessons learned.
- Love yourself first, as this is the key to attracting real unconditional love in your life (it does exist because I have found it, and so can you).
- Be grateful for everything in your life and acknowledge this daily, for it will create more abundance.
- You are safe, protected and always provided for.
- Your passed loved ones and spirit team are closer than you think. You can learn to communicate with them to assist you on your journey.
- Follow the breadcrumbs in life. They will lead you to your most abundant path.
- Reach out to others that are on a different vibrational level so that they may guide you (it'll make your journey a lot easier).
- Everything is energy, including your thoughts, so create the most expansive thought system possible.
- Believe that you have access to your most abundant timeline and take steps to experience it.
- Your triggers point you to what you still need to heal.
- Trust your intuition and always listen to your soul; it will NEVER steer you wrong.
- Explore, learn, and continue to strive to become your highest self.
- What you want exists... don't settle.
- Forgive.
- Love.

- LIVE!

Thank you for being part of my journey. My intention for this chapter was to provide you with inspiration and hope... to acknowledge that you are NEVER stuck in life. I hope that you saw yourself somewhere in me along my journey and that you know that if it's possible for me to break free from a belief system that I held for fifty years, it is also possible for you!

You are the creator of your journey... make it an amazing one!

Sending you much love and gratitude!

ABOUT THE AUTHOR
JUDY LYNN MITCHELL

Judy is a manifestation coach and ascension guide and founder of Holistic Modalities. She helps women elevate their consciousness from feeling lost and stuck to awakening their inner power to magnetize and create their desires by clearing limiting beliefs/fears, releasing old perceptions and creating a new expansive thought system.

She is a Usui Reiki master, Rahanni practitioner and certified Akashic Records practitioner. She uses her gifts of channelling and energy work to take others to the next level of who they are and teaches them her specific channelled methods to consciously create their desires.

Her vision is to inspire other women to find their voices, to believe in themselves and to know that what they wish to create is only a belief away.

She recently moved back to the country in Alberta, Canada, with her beautiful daughter Hailey, her soulmate Wayne and their three dogs to be surrounded by the abundance of nature.

Website: *https://www.holisticmodalities.ca*
Instagram: *https://www.instagram.com/judy.holistic.modalities*
Personal Facebook Page: *https://www.facebook.com/Judy.Mitchell09*
Facebook Business Page:
https://www.facebook.com/judyholisticmodalities
Facebook Group:
https://www.facebook.com/groups/2485224008364986/?source_id=345518846072065

LinkedIn: *https://www.linkedin.com/in/judy-lynn-047689135*
Email: *jl.holistic.modalities@gmail.com*

LISA ÉVOLUER

FROM THE SUPERFICIAL ADVERTISING WORLD TO SPIRITUAL FREEDOM

Do you wake up every day feeling full of energy and present in the moment without thinking of your to-do list? Do you love yourself when you look in the mirror? Do you speak your truth without being afraid of what others might think of you and whether you would be accepted?

There have been times I haven't felt like this...

I was on my laptop on a warm summer day, trying to proceed with a project I'd been charged with. All of a sudden, I felt this burst of energy inside of me and the urge to run away from my laptop. My eyes started to fill with tears. I could not take it anymore. I had to get up and get away from this laptop. I fled to the bedroom, feeling the cold tiles underneath my feet, and slid down the wardrobe until I sat on the ground.

While it was warm and sunny outside, with a crystal clear, tranquil sea, there was an autumn storm raging inside of me. I knew I had to get away from this job and the people that came with it. The superficial advertising industry—people not appreciating me for who I was, but only for the work I did. My job felt meaningless. I was burned out, and I felt empty inside.

It was a situation I knew all too well from when I quit my apprenticeship as a graphic designer. At that time, I thought everyone else except me was successful and happy. I was afraid of what my parents and friends would think of me for quitting my job. Back then, everything was too much; every noise felt like it would suffocate me. I knew I had to quit, but I was afraid of being dependent on my boyfriend until I would make enough money on my own.

There was a similar situation just a few years later. We had just moved to Malta to start our new life there—at a sunny place with the deep blue sea just minutes away from our home—when I realized that I could not work there as a makeup artist because the mentality and beauty ideals of the locals were completely different to mine. For weeks, I was hiding in bed, watching meaningless series... I even wanted to convince my boyfriend to end our relationship because I did not want to burden him.

And there I was, just two years later... Sitting on the cold tiles with this autumn storm raging inside of me. This time it was different. I knew there was a way out because I had already been through this situation twice. At this moment, I just didn't know what this way out would look like.

No one except my boyfriend knew how I felt—I was pretty good at hiding my feelings, always seeming to be a reliable rock to lean on for others.

One of my mentors likes to say: "Sometimes we have to go very deep underwater to be able to ride the wave of joy."

This storm had started to rise a while ago; I just didn't see it coming. I remembered how people tried to push me and wanted to keep me going, although my boyfriend had just been diagnosed with a tumor after years of suffering and suddenly had to undergo emergency surgery. Some of my clients did not want to accept I needed a break and kept messaging me, telling me I was unprofessional even though I recommended other retouchers to them. When I broke several bones in my wrist just a few months later, I was forced to take a break for a couple of months. I was afraid to lose my income that I needed to start from scratch again...

Not being able to work meant a lot of "me-time". Time to think about myself and how I had changed over the past years. Accepting I did not want to continue working like this.

A couple of weeks later, I found myself on a plane to Mallorca to visit a so-called "business-bootcamp". On the first day, our mentor looked into the eyes of each participant and asked a very insightful question: "If you had enough money to live as you wish and didn't have to work anymore, would you still want to do what you're currently doing?" Immediately, I could hear myself screaming "No!" inside of my head.

I decided it was time to quit and rediscover who I was and what was truly important to me. I achieved everything an aspiring retoucher wanted to achieve; however, it did not make me truly happy. The feeling of fulfillment, a feeling of peace and gratefulness, was missing

Today I know it was because I was only chasing achievements society rated as being successful. However, we can only achieve true fulfillment when being motivated by our inner force, living aligned with our values.

I went on a six-month break, did lots of yoga, tried freediving and worked in my friends diving school for fun—being around all these different people and spending a lot of time practising yoga helped me to see things more clearly. I loved how these people got along with each other without bragging about achievements, without trying to put a mask on. Everyone was so real... Something very different to the advertising industry.

I wanted to get away from this fake world. Work with "real" people. People who didn't only look for outer beauty, but wanted to make the world a better place, by empowering others to not just chase outer success, but inner fulfillment. All that was missing was finding out who I was first and finding my own fulfillment.

When I attended my first yoga class, I remembered that as a child, my father told me it was a weird hippie thing and everything about psychology was something for losers. As a teenager, I hid all books about spirituality so my parents or friends would not find out I was interested in "woo" things to not think of me as some maniac. All this led to me putting on masks... Putting on layers since I did not feel accepted for who I was and being insecure in my own body. I straightened my hair since other girls in school had this perfect, shiny, straight hair. I put on layers of makeup every day for years without questioning why. My work as a makeup artist supported this even more until I was completely numb, functioning like a robot.

I did not have any recurring income during this time, but I knew it was the right decision.

My boyfriend and I created my membership site so that I was able to sell my online course. It should be a final "bundle" for my community, all my knowledge as a "goodbye offer" before quitting the retouching industry.

Yoga, freediving and attending a course to learn about mindfulness helped me rediscover who I was. Suddenly, even the artist name I chose years ago made sense.

When working as a makeup artist, I changed my surname to Évoluer so my last name would not be that of a drugstore chain in Germany. After all, it was all about status in this scene. Now that I transformed myself, broke out of the superficial world and discovered a spiritual path, the name started to form a deeper meaning.

That was the moment where the magic started to happen.

Working on my membership site ignited the spark in Dennis and me to offer the solution of an easy membership site to others. We wanted to support other coaches to easily share their knowledge. It was the key moment in which our company Coachy started to form itself.

This also led to my boyfriend becoming even more unhappy at work... He saw me being grounded and happy about my decision to quit my retouching business while he was still stuck in his underpaid full-time job. One day, he felt completely drained, and I empowered him to quit.

There we were. With just a few savings, an idea and only months away from moving into our own flat, for which we still needed to buy furniture.

What others would have seen as crazy was crystal clear for us. We wanted to follow our passion and we had a deep feeling of trust as a result of all the previous years. Everything would work out.

We knew we had to limit ourselves financially but that it would be worth it. We could do what we were truly passionate about.

This was 2017. We knew we created something amazing. However, we would have never imagined how fast our idea would grow into an industry-leading platform with a team behind it.

We created this business not only to help people not feel overwhelmed by technical hurdles and help them to focus on their coaching business, but also that we could be more independent ourselves.

Unfortunately, our success turned into the exact opposite after just a couple of months. We had replaced the dream of freedom with a hamster wheel. Especially my boyfriend, who was very new to being self-employed, worked from morning until bedtime, only taking breaks to eat.

When you constantly work because otherwise the amount of work will overwhelm you or your subconscious is trying to prove something by being busy all the time, not only your body will suffer from it.

The pressure we feel within ourselves will grow endlessly. Relationships will suffer. That's what happened to us, and I know that many other people—whether self-employed or employed—suffer similarly.

I knew how to consciously take breaks to take a walk with our dog, do yoga or go for a swim; it became really hard to get Dennis out of his software development "tunnel". It felt as if we were still living in the same apartment and were working on the same business, but our relationship turned into a work relationship. As a couple, a true relationship goes far beyond working together in business. No matter how much you love your job or business, it's so important to still have a life apart from it—time for friends, family, hobbies and other fun activities that make us feel inspired and energized.

The constant pressure and unhappiness put a strain on our relationship.

Absence of a real plan and the fact we were just doing something for the sake of doing things dragged us further into the abyss. I knew it could not go on like this. The problem was not only within us, but also was created from the outside—by our surroundings.

Your social environment often has different beliefs, ideas and a view of life. Other people have different values, whether they are truly theirs or have been passed on to them by parents and other people close to them. Through those values and experiences, they create a reality that is different from ours. Even if they do not mean to cause any harm, they are not you.

Although working with our business partner, who came on board to focus on marketing in late summer 2017, went well, it got harder and harder as our business kept on growing fast.

We wanted to search for employees who could support us, manage themselves and shared the same vision and had the necessary skills. Our business partner wanted to hire virtual assistants here and there—who did not have the skills or totally different values.

We wanted to take breaks to rest, create a stable structure for more focus and sustainable growth; he wanted to push sales and other things spontaneously.

I felt angry and frustrated and I didn't understand him since I like honest people whose actions match their words. He told us he wasn't only in it for the money, but he proved otherwise as he constantly chased after more. Whether it was his inner insecurity and lack of money in the past or just greed, we never found out.

In 2019, it was time to make a cut and truly shift the focus from working all the time to living a true, self-determined life in freedom.

We decided to separate from our business partner and move to a different country. We did not only want a business, but also to be surrounded by an environment matching our values.

At this time, we felt overwhelmed, frustrated... I was more and more worried about our dog's safety since, over the years, the island where we lived got more crowded, and there was less nature left to take walks. It also meant that the aggressive hunters had less space, and we constantly bumped into them on our walks. I remember one time I complained about a hunter who was shooting in a nature reserve, and he grabbed me on my shirt, shouted at me and then chased after me. Another time, we went on a hiking trail, and my boyfriend's brother got off the trail. Immediately, a hunter came shouting at us with his rifle in his hand. It told him I'd call the police, and he just told me to 'fuck off' and I, the 'whore', shouldn't dare to call the police.

Even friends got thrown stones after them, got tires pricked and their children bullied at school. Tourists and locals sometimes got accidentally wounded by a shot, but the press always hid the accidents. Even among the police and politicians, there were people that were part of the hunting lobby.

On such a tiny island, everyone knows everyone, so I started to always look behind me when taking walks alone.

Everything in our life felt messy, but we did not give up. Thankfully, I discovered yoga and mindfulness to give me the ability to calm down and feel at peace whenever I needed some grounding. It made me feel safe.

While we were desperately looking for another place to move to, we attended the International Yoga Day on the summer solstice and got introduced to Kundalini yoga.

I remember the teacher asking us to set an intention and at some point ask the universe for the answers we were looking for.

A picture started to form in front of my closed eyes as I was sitting there with closed eyes, on top of a hill in an old fort, feeling the summer breeze and taking deep breaths during meditation. I saw sparkling, turquoise water. A golden beach and a very specific rock formation made of limestone. It felt as if I was standing on a cliff, looking at a beach and the rock formation, hearing the soft waves washing on shore. I knew immediately that this had to be the place where we were supposed to go. However, at that time, I had no idea where it was supposed to be.

Back at home, I began digging, trying to find someplace without aggressive hunters—somewhere around the Mediterranean—with lots of nature, where we would be able to manage to live without speaking the language right from the start.

There was only one country that ticked all the boxes. Portugal.

I quickly checked which ferry we could take to the mainland, so we would be able to take the car. I found out there was only one spot left—in three weeks. Otherwise, we would have to wait until late autumn. Having experienced many storms in autumn where ferries weren't able to pass, we knew we either had to leave in three weeks or wait until spring the following year. At this point, no one could have known it was the best timing for us because just half a year, later the pandemic happened, and we would have been stuck in Italy.

We focused on packing our stuff, making sure our apartment was ready to get sold and that our business kept running, without us doing much!

That was when we realized we already had a secure and stable base with our business—it kept growing, without planning campaigns and sales, events or working on it daily.

From this moment on, we focused on setting up structures and processes for our company and hiring team members who share the same values.

Since then, we were able to run a business with a team that is on fire. A business based on clear values and systems profiting from the possibilities of the digital world. A company that grows sustainably and with fun, ease and flow.

For a fulfilled and relaxed life, matching our values of independence, sustainability, financial freedom, empowering others and authenticity.

Today, I am still co-founder of our company, but the team and systems we've implemented give me freedom, so I am able to follow my passion to empower and guide women to rise.

I'm here to guide you when you are feeling out of alignment and help you rediscover your true self, burst through limiting beliefs and step into your own power. So you have a deep feeling of gratitude and know connecting to spirit is not weird or "woo-woo", but a choice of breaking free. For being able to live your most abundant, relaxed and successful life—aligned to your values.

I am a huge fan of combining neuroscience with ancient wisdom within my work—Human Design, Kundalini and Mindfulness.

It's time to break free and live your life as YOU want to live it; in ease, fun and flow. Tear off your mask, and let's unleash your magical gift!

Let's live a magical and adventurous life.
BE. wild. real. free.

ABOUT THE AUTHOR
LISA ÉVOLUER

Lisa Évoluer is Co-Founder of Coachy®, entrepreneur, Kundalini business coach, published author and yogini. She founded the industry-leading seven-figure company Coachy with her boyfriend and loves supporting women to rise, having broken free from working in the superficial advertising field herself.

Her work guides ambitious businesswomen from feeling out of alignment to re-discover themselves, bust through limiting beliefs and step into their own power to be able to live their most abundant and successful life. Lisa combines neuroscience with ancient wisdom - Human Design, Kundalini and Mindfulness. One of her mottos is "Let's live our life with more fun, ease and flow! BE. Wild. Authentic. Free: BOLD."

She wants to raise awareness of living more sustainably by protecting nature and empower women. Born in Germany, she lives in Portugal with her boyfriend and her dog.

Updates & all links in one: *https://go.lisa-evoluer.com/letsconnect*
Free 60-minute workshop: *http://lisa-evoluer.coachy.net/lp/workshop*
Website: *www.lisa-evoluer.com*
Company: *www.coachy.net*
Instagram: *https://www.instagram.com/lisaevoluer*
YouTube: *https://www.youtube.com/user/LisaEvoluer*

MATHILDE ANGLADE

DARING TO BE GREAT, OR A STORY ON CHOICE AND BELIEF USING LAND AS A PORTAL

This story is potent. It is infused with spells of love, strength, and wisdom and holds shamanic and royal medicine. This story comes from my womb and pours out of my throat. It is a portal of expansion that I gift to you. May it make your soul sing.

***

Teenage Mathilde, posters of *Buffy*, *Charmed*, *Alias*, and other badass actresses are the wallpaper of my bedroom walls, door and ceiling—not an inch is left untouched. Family lunch at home. As usual, the intensity of my bedroom causes comments and smiles. I hear my parents: "Roooooo, it's just a phase, she's going to grow up". Ouch.

A small yet defining moment. Time stops. An unconscious narrative takes over: "I want my parents to love and respect me, to take me seriously". Danger zone. Two weeks later, my bedroom is blank. I told my soul to stop singing and colouring the world. I kicked her out of my body. Why? A lack of sovereignty. One of many instances.

I tie a muzzle on my creativity, my spirit. I get on the pill, and I quit dance performances, painting classes with my mum, and playing the piano. I am top of the class at school even though I am bored and sit at the back of the class chatting. It buys me perceived freedom. I get into the best business school in France and get a license in applied mathematics on the side. I have fun, I have friends, I party, I travel, I laugh. Life is really good. The problem? I haven't let those parts of my soul back in yet. I am not fully running the show; my traumatised human is.

*

2014, Australia, bathroom. Far away from intense France, I see myself in the mirror. Perplexed, I look at myself see myself. "Being human is trippy. I don't feel like this is me"—the disconnection between my body and my soul. My soul is not welcome in this body. It is such that physical death has to be next, my soul wanting a vessel to express itself through. I ride my scooter, pondering on whether or not I should sharply turn the handlebar.

I dismantle my life in search of this anchoring in self I used to feel. In search of loving life instead of liking it. I want more. I stop the pill, and with it goes away depression, migraines, and disconnection from my body almost instantly. I break up with my boyfriend and change employer. Today, I have understood that my Kali doesn't need to destroy everything in my physical world. Back then, I didn't know. Left with myself and using the Australian land as a spiritual portal to go inwards, I can dive inside and hear my soul from the faraway place I cast her to.

2015, in bed, morning after a cocaine-fuelled night in Bondi Beach, the most profound thing happens. I decide that it is enough. From the depth of my guts: "I am going to be happy now". The boldest and most loving choice I ever made. I surprise myself as I say those words as if, for the first time, I realised I had the power to choose. A rush of energy rises in me. My state of being changes. This is the moment I consciously chose life.

*

I realise that I was born in this world and never asked if I wanted to be here. I just was. I had made the decision not to die, not the decision to live. That morning, I discovered the power of choice and commitment to letting life live in me.

Have you consciously chosen life?

*

Let's pause. Isn't it such a gift this ability we have to make choices and go on different paths? Literally every single moment is a door to a new world. What am I choosing in this moment? I am choosing the expansion and the unknown through expression of my soul in this book. This moment opened the door to a world with more books and more soul expression for me and for you by reading this.

***

This choice became the bedrock of a tsunami of self-love and the permission-giver to my quest for passion, purpose, and alignment. After creating a beautifully formatted Excel document (the deepest joy of my corporate career) where I analysed my career choices, desires, regrets, and reasons for not following my clean desires and intuition, I remember I want to make the world a better place. The night before the deadline to accept a position in a Master's of

Security and Intelligence in London, I have a dream: "No, this isn't how you want to live". I refuse the offer.

*

Something critical happens here—another decision point. I realise my power. On a quest to make the world a better place where everyone is loved and respected in their expression, after working for non-profit clients and heading towards an international conflict resolution career, I realise I am missing the point! I am putting to the side the most powerful agent for change in my possession, me. The soul-expressed me, not the smart, degree-abundant, on train tracks me. The real, alive me. I realise that what is egotistic is this perceived selflessness where I make people around me more important and let them take my power away, which ironically prevents me from purely loving them because I cannot see their real selves either. I choose myself and realise how huge of a difference it makes in the world what state I am in. The best way to make the world a better place is to do something I truly love and let this love ripple. I choose to make the world a better place by committing to living in a state of love and joy through the portal of doing what I love.

Where does it lead me? The trance of acting. Scrolling through Instagram, a moment of heightened awareness. I realise actors are... human beings. The end of the pedestal—an imperative step to be who I desire to be. Two days later, I am on the set of the TV series *Top of the Lake*, looking at Elizabeth Moss and Nicole Kidman act, and the crew do their magic. A moment of grace. Time slows down again. Joy this time. Not my everyday human joy. A deep, rooted, slow joy. 'This is home'. A part of my soul lights back up. Choosing myself and love was necessary to receive more of my soul. It was the requirement for my soul to feel safe in me.

From then on, divine joy is the state I live in. I forgive myself and discover kindness and compassion. I follow the joy wherever it takes me. Following my intuition and doing what I love is my only rule. I quit my corporate job. Friends call me 'brave' and 'risk taking'. This is the easiest decision of my life. I don't understand that it can seem brave and risky to others. My soul is running the show.

*

Acting becomes my spiritual practice. Joy and alignment become my purpose, along with helping others feel free to feel, expressed, and loved, through my art. And, it does ripple. I bring joy everywhere I go. I inspire friends whose soul desires to sing more too. I become an activator of alignment and purpose. I lift the energy everywhere I go, one smile at a time. I don't try; it is my state. I find ecstasy and tears looking at a traffic light because I feel humanity's desire for safety and creation. I experience joy as someone unleashes at me on the road because I see the beauty of the human experience. For years, I cannot help but see beauty and feel compassion. Peace.

Have you accepted that you are as powerful as what you put on a pedestal?

*

Let's pause. Isn't it weird that right now I am writing and you are reading my story? This ability we have to explore ourselves is trippy as fuck. Isn't it weird how we humans are fascinated by ourselves and each other? Aren't we the cutest thing? Big teddy bears who want to know about each other, be happy and have a great life? We make films, music, sit at dinner tables together even when it's hard, text each other, go dancing, or simply sit next to each other in silence. The relationship I have with myself, others, and life, is here. It won't go away. I can choose to make it toxic or healthy. Might as well make it feel as beautiful as possible, right?

***

2018, walking in my bedroom. A voice says: "It's time to go back down; there is more". Down where? More what? Is it intuition? Is it the voice of the ego bored of peace and wanting drama? Is it the voice of wisdom that knows that all is unknown and infinite? Do I believe that is it my human ego because I don't believe in my state of divine love? Do I believe that it is my wise intuition because I don't want to admit that it is my ego? An endless spiral of thought can open here. Stop. I breathe.

What feels beautiful? Wise? Fun? I listen hard. Once I choose, I will commit because I know that if it is a call for expansion, my human will barge in to try and make me go the other way because it does not want to die. I remember that the commitment to my choice and belief in myself are the secret to my expansion when I am in the human alchemy of it all.

"Let's do it. Let's leave this state and go into the unknown". The frequency shifts. The ceremony starts. My inner witch desires to go into my lower chakras. I signal the beginning of journeying into my dark feminine and womb. I will find increased wisdom, rooted in the Earth this time, instead of in the crown.

*

Me too movement. I am triggered. I find excuses. "It wasn't that bad". "Some people have it worse". "Maybe it didn't happen". "Maybe I'm crazy". "I could have fought back more, so maybe it's my fault". Do we all realise the sadness of this thought? "I could have fought back more, so maybe it's my fault".

I admit the stories my subconscious wrote to protect me. I find the courage to rewrite them. Am I allowed to change stories of the past? Yes. I must, in fact. As I raised my frequency, expanded my mind, and healed my heart, I got to rewrite the past from a new state. Those times where once again, I let my soul leave my body—golden sparkles flying in the air from lifeless eyes. I forgive myself and others. Where does it lead me? Receiving more of my soul.

Sexual attacks were the most effective way to enslave my body. Why? Because it took over its most sacred space, like a missionary erecting a church over sacred land. The darkness of these experiences made it hard for my mind to understand what was happening when it did. Now, I understand why my female organs are sacred. They are basecamp for the power of creation itself. I pray for all to find reverence.

This took a lot of healing. It took me believing in my temple and silencing the mocking voices of uncomfortable humans. I embodied the indigenous European Earth woman I grew up as and took myself inside in the dark to hold this nugget of sacredness in this war field. Faith, belief, and an undying commitment to life being my guides, one moment after another.

What stories do you need to rewrite?

*

Let's pause. What was happening on a cosmic level? Since the youngest age, I was receiving nudges, invitations to expand my voice. Often in the form of caging it. Every time I didn't choose freedom of the soul, the universe sent me/I gathered for myself stronger challenges, which resulted in trauma when I didn't choose expansion. Sometimes, I didn't have the expanded consciousness, the healed heart, and the open mind to understand the invitation. Hence why I keep walking this path, looking for the invitations I create for myself.

***

2019, I move to Los Angeles, where the authenticity and reclamation of my voice are amplified by the portal that the South Californian land is. Six months earlier, I make another energetic decision—to open myself where resistance ruled: deeper intimacy with male humans. The energy shifts. Soon, I meet my powerful magician, my intuitive lover, my King, Bradley. His strength, presence, and beautiful masculine energy invites me to drop deeper into my feminine. We dance together. The ceremony has begun. This time, I am ready to be in it with someone. Deep healing takes place. Sometimes feeling like starting from scratch. A whole new layer of the onion. Gratitude is my door to seeing the invitations. Co-dependency nudges invite me into more sovereignty. Anxious attachment nudges invite me into new layers of self-love and power. Belief is my lighthouse.

*

Starry sky forest. I am sitting with Ayahuasca and my beloved. The medicine goes up and down from my womb to my throat, offering decision points: "Do this or I will purge it". "Scream". I scream. "Speak". I scream: "I don't know what to say". That night, it is harder to scream than usual. It is stuck in my womb. She continues coming up my throat, wanting to purge the trauma out of my body. I am determined and fierce. I want to consciously work with her in the middle world. I realise I have to say it, scream it. Oh god. Fear. Let's do it. I scream: "I have been raped, multiple times, and I can say it", reconnecting my womb and my voice.

*

Nine months later, I release a timeline of queen persecution and a karmic bond with my king through hypnosis. I catapult to a past life as an Egyptian queen. Lying on a stone table, tied up and strangled for speaking powerful words, three men on each side and one at the back, his hands on my temples. Is he invading my thoughts? No. He is shrinking my golden halo. My hypnosis oracle says: "Sometimes people want to tear down the queen". It sinks in. It is time to receive the seed of discernment. I shrink the man until he disappears, removing this from being acceptable in my psyche. Back home, my partner says: "I visited the same place during a medicine journey. I always wondered what was on the table because I was too small to see". Chills. Pause. Deep breath. I realise the powerful karmic bond of persecution we both healed. Purification.

*

Let's pause. Does my mind want to reduce these experiences sometimes? Yes. "It's just imagination". My mind is scared of the greatness of life and of believing. Thank you, mind. I don't need it. It does nothing for me except protect me against...what? Disappointment? That what? That maybe none of this is true? Well, my dear Mathilde, let's make one thing clear, you don't know anything. The idea of knowledge is a trap for the wisdom of my soul. So what do I do? I choose the story that breathes beauty. The story that feels as if life and beauty are blooming out of me. Beauty—the door to my soul.

***

Today, I share my medicine in the movies I act in, the words I weave together, and in the music I create. I believe in a kind and beautiful world populated by soul-expressed and sovereign beings.

I live life as a ceremony and lead my projects as such. I own my greatness. I own that my presence and expression are a gift to this world. I intend to receive as much of my soul as possible to pour this divine expression into the world and create beauty, kindness, and love whilst having fun. Why? Because it feels great.

I am a leader changing the structure of my industries, weaving in my witchcraft and shamanic practices, which creates a unique expression that my clients are magnetised by across the world. My clients and team are the big hearts of film directors, writers, producers, musicians, photographers, artists, and above all, believers in magic. Together we make magic by bringing our soul into what we birth. We create art that cannot be fully explained, art that touches the divine humanity in us, hoping to make your soul sing too.

*

Let's pause. I have decided to make the best out of this weird thing that life is. Life is so fucking weird! Let's not pretend it's not the maddest thing ever. I have no idea about anything that's going on here either. We believe that we are orbiting around the sun because science proved it. God knows what science will prove in ten thousand years. Fascinating and wiiiiild. So. I have decided to create my world and play. I have decided to believe. In what? Just to believe. My soul feels it. I have chosen love, kindness, beauty, joy and soul expression. Yes, the road is bumpy, and what a hell of a fun ride this is. Isn't it? If I had to remember one thing for my next life, it would be: "Do yoga and put your feet on the Earth". For now, I live to love myself and others on my death bed. Catch you on the other side, beautiful.

***

Thank you for reading my story.
With love,

Mathilde.

ABOUT THE AUTHOR
MATHILDE ANGLADE

Mathilde is a French-Australian actress, writer and music performer.

You can watch Mathilde's stellar performance in her directorial debut *The Corners of Your Smile* on Vimeo On Demand. A beautiful love story between two women that will touch your human heart and remind you of the greyness of life and the importance of love, forgiveness, and expression.

For Mathilde's music, follow her on Spotify and YouTube to catch her new release on the August 8th Leo new moon—this piece will take you through an ethereal and shamanic journey of creation, following a cosmic alien spirit diving into nature and the womb of creation to birth integrated heart-fulled beauty.

To create magic with her, head over to her website or Instagram page.

Website: www.mathildeanglade.com
Instagram: https://www.instagram.com/mathilde_anglade/
Film: https://vimeo.com/ondemand/thecornersofyoursmile
YouTube: https://tinyurl.com/2stbka97
Spotify: https://tinyurl.com/4p7smhyh

PHOEBE LEONA

A STORY OF CO-CREATION WITH CHAOS

As a child, I intuitively felt that societal paths that were predetermined and conditioned only initiated a disconnection from self, which generated inner chaos filled with questions, doubts, and fears, so fortunately for me, I never felt swayed by them. When people asked me what I wanted to be when I grew up, I would respond without any hesitation, "a choreographer!" I was never attached to what that would look like, and I didn't have any kind of vision of having a husband, children, or a big home. I simply just wanted to create dances, and I pretty much stayed the course. I was lucky enough that no one in my immediate world ever questioned or doubted me or instilled any kind of fear in me that it was impossible. In fact, it was just the opposite for me, and if anyone did, I never saw it or never engaged with it a way that I ever gave it a second thought.

I also learned at a very young age that chaos is an act of creation, and for a period of my life, I believed it was the act of my own creation rather than a co-creation, which scared me. My story comes from the chaos created on the outside that questioned the power of my intuition, my inner voice. My hope for you is that by the end of my story, you will feel that no matter where the chaos is born from; the disorder of your internal world or external world, that you always have the ability to see it for what it is and choose to engage with it as you wish and embrace your life as a co-creator.

We begin with my parents, who met one day in the mid-70s while my dad was out walking one of his pet lions—yes, *one* of his pet lions; remember this was the 70s. He was walking his lion, Simba, out on the leash through the streets of York, PA, while my mom, a young impressionable college student, was waiting for her bus. She saw Dad and Simba and began to flirt with Dad. There was a party involved, and the rest of that story is what made my history. At the time, Dad was the owner of a waterbed store and a pretty successful drug dealer. He also suffered from shellshock—that is what they called PTSD back then—from his two tours in Vietnam. Dad was a man of chaos, in all the ways; good, wild, bad, and ugly.

My very early years were relatively happy, and I felt very loved. When I was seven, my parents split up and things shifted. I stayed living with Dad, who, by that time, had changed careers to senior computer programmer and was doing rather well for himself. Mom thought it would be best for me to stay in my home, in my school with my friends, and with Dad to keep us both on a steady path. She thought if he was responsible for me and stayed with his responsible job, all of his internal chaos would disappear. It didn't.

The divorce crushed Dad, and his rage became unbearable for all parties involved. I watched him beat up my mom, his girlfriend, and I came in the line of fire a couple times which thankfully only involved me being thrown into walls and piles of sticks on a few occasions. His nine-to-five job came home with him on the weekends and late nights, which also became detrimental to his mental health. He would tell me how he wanted to jump out the window of his office and climb the walls to be free, even though he was extremely intelligent and very successful at what he did. I always thought it was ironic that he worked in a big office building with rooms filled with motherboard computers for an organization called the Nature Conservancy. His drug use became a threat to everyone's lives, especially his own when we had to check him into rehab after an attempted suicide. My home life was utter chaos. Moments of joy wrapped intimately with moments of hysteria that held screaming, crying, hugging, slamming doors, police visits, dancing, hospital waiting rooms, singing, threats, laughing, and violence all within a blink of an eye.

It felt chaotic, but at the same time, I always knew *it* was about to happen. I felt the shifts of energy, the change of the wind, the look in his eye, the song that came on that triggered a mood, and snap, it all happened. I felt crazy because I sensed these things before they happened, and I believed that I made them happen, even on that day he almost killed Mom. I had been mad at her for leaving us, when she came to our door to see me, madness broke out within seconds, a literal car chase through suburban Maryland where I was the bait, and ended at my dad's friend's house in a cloud of pot smoke and Dad handing him a gun saying, "Please take this, I almost used it today." I actually believed for years that I was the one who almost killed my mom through my own thoughts and feelings.

I continuously felt that I was making the chaos happen in my outer world, and at some point, I turned it off. At least, that is what I thought. The rush of chaos still came to me through the excitement and passion for boys, living in the city, and my dance career. I rode the waves of the highs and lows and unconsciously searched them out, calling it "magic." What I had actually turned off was my intuition, that inner voice, even though it stayed close by and still told me to look out, I just didn't listen too well. I ignored it and pretended to be shocked when the worst happened, so I could just be the victim, not the villain that created the chaos. It wasn't until I lost everything that I began to really listen again.

When I was fifteen, I left Dad because I could not take the pain of watching him relapse over and over again at the expense of my own mental wellness. He disappeared shortly after my departure; evicted from our home, homeless, arrested, and dead were all possibilities, for all I knew. He didn't show up again until seventeen years later when I learned that all those things happened, including a very close declaration of his death.

In that time in between for me, I lived in New York City, fulfilled my dream as a dancer, became a yoga teacher, and got married to my college boyfriend—a man that mirrored my dad in many ways, including the chaos. I was happy to a certain extent, but there was a darkness lurking underneath my marriage; the pressures of life as artists, fulfilling our dreams, compromising our dreams, his drinking and drug use, both of us being workaholics, and my loneliness.

In the spring of 2009, when we were trying to fix things between us, I had a reoccurring dream of me outside my childhood home with my friends, family, and husband. We were all waiting for the arrival of Dad. Finally, he pulled up and jumped out of a car wearing an EMT coat. We all celebrated and hugged except my husband, who stood off to the side, just staring at us with this look of disconnection.

A couple months later, out of "nowhere" on Father's Day, Dad called me and announced he was sober, rehabbed, and wanted to be in my life again. It was a magical reunion, and somehow, at least for me, it repaired all the other problems, both my marriage and my life. The following year, we moved out of the city to be closer to my dad and set better boundaries for my husband's work.

By spring of 2012, we moved into our dream home as first-time homeowners, and I got a full-time gig running my own yoga program. Everything was "perfect." I somehow fell into the American Dream without setting that intention or being aware of it until the day I was literally painting my white picket fence. The only moment I felt a real pang of anxiety was when we went to sign the mortgage, those many pages stating that my life would be at one residence for the next thirty years. It felt dreadful knowing that, even though it was a home I loved. When I lived in the city, I believed I would live there all of my life, but no one ever had me sign anything to keep that promise. I just felt caged in.

That summer, my husband and I went to a baseball game across the river. We ran into his co-worker, whose personal life he seemed to know a lot about. I didn't really care but just annoyed that we had to make small talk with her and her boyfriend since they seemed so much younger and immature. They left a little early since the boyfriend was in charge of the fireworks, being a firefighter at the local fire department.

The fireworks were enjoyable to watch but the smoke caused a severe reaction in my lungs. Just getting over a small summer cold, I began to cough uncontrollably to the point I thought I was having an asthma attack. I didn't have asthma, never had asthma. I was bright red and struggled to breathe. My husband asked me if I wanted him to take me to the ER. I squeaked out "no" and somehow regained composure halfway across the river on our way back home. That night I felt it was imperative to insist on making love to my husband, even though it had been months for us. I went on to having bronchitis for the next four months. I finally kicked it right before Christmas, which ended up being a moment I would look back on for many years, as being the first and last Christmas, of being in my dream home, with my dad and husband.

A couple weeks later, in January, Dad died in his sleep. Two months later, my husband asked for a divorce after fifteen years together, one reason being that he was having an affair with the co-worker from the baseball game months prior. In the midst of my shock and grief, I went to see an acupuncturist. She asked me when I had bronchitis that I had checked off on my chart. I replied, "Last summer and fall, why?" She looked at me, laid her hand on my hand and said, "My dear, your body was grieving this whole time. Your body knew!" She then explained how in Chinese medicine, grief is carried and expressed in the lungs.

That is the moment I began to wake up again. I began to look back at all of my dreams, journals, feelings, inklings of knowing, illnesses, and all the other messages I had ignored over the years. I began to realize that my intuition was present the whole time, keeping a third eye on chaos while I just looked the other way and slept. For the rest of 2013, I kept my eyes wide open, all three of them, as I watched what was left of my life deconstruct before me. I lost the home, my dog that I had to put to sleep, and my own health, which was deteriorating. Chaos came through like a tornado and left me with the best thing that could have ever happen to me, a breakthrough.

I woke up one morning in October and didn't recognize myself in the mirror. The day my boss told me that I was failing at my job because my grieving was taking too long and told by a lab technician that I probably could not have kids because of what she saw on my ultrasound. Both things I didn't have any energy to care about, but I was sick of life telling me, "No", I was "failing", or I "can't have" anymore. It was time to take control back to my life.

I texted my mom that I wanted to come home, and she simply replied, "Come home, Phoebe" I cancelled my classes and drove five hours to my mom's. On my drive, I cried, screamed, sang, and thought deeply about what the hell I was going to do next. I heard a voice.

It was a familiar voice. It whispered to leave my job and start my own business. The only thing I had was a minimal amount of inheritance from my dad coming to me. So on the other side of my five-hour drive, I had a plan to sublet my apartment, leave my job, and start a new life somewhere that was not yet to be determined. With my mom's support, I took action after a couple days of recovery. I did everything I set out to do within a month, and my little voice that I was starting to listen to again, led me to Costa Rica where I lived for nine months to rest, recover, and build my business to support people through their own transformation. After nine months and the small savings I still had, I came back to launch my business in the Hudson Valley. I had connections there and knew I could get work and students fast to grow my following for retreats. Every step I took with trust in my inner voice, a new step was revealed, and another, and then another. After my launch of nOMad, I grew our community beyond the Hudson Valley, beyond retreats to community events, teacher trainings, a podcast, an online membership program, and even back to my very first dream.

My inner voice again led me back to dancing. I found I was moving my body in a way to heal it and help heal others through my somatic movement/dance practice, Mvt109™, that I intuitively developed with a healer. It led me to trust that voice again through new choices of relationships, potentially dangerous situations, business decisions, and where I would end up during the pandemic. It kept me safe, and since our relationship has strengthened, the chaos has quieted considerably.

I say this now as we all collectively are going through the most chaotic times of our lifetime: I feel safe and grounded more than I have ever felt before. I was in Bali up until March 18, 2020. As I laid in a breathwork session and asked the question, "what do I do next?" I saw a vision of Mom and Gramma and heard, "go home, Phoebe." So I did. I went to West Virginia, a place I never called home but calling me back and became closer with my family than I had ever been. I healed old wounds that I didn't even know were there. I went deeply inward as the world spun out of control through Covid, protests, riots, elections, shootings, and threats of a civil war. I held my ground because I kept hearing a voice within saying, "Trust", and so I have listened, and I continue to listen, and now I have arrived in a place that I never even thought I could imagine, Peace.

Over the last year, chaos was all around me, screaming through the TV some days and brought me the news of the passing of my childhood best friend who was like a sister to me, something that I sensed was coming just days before. It was all around and up close and personal. I saw it, noticed it, I felt it, and I chose not to engage with it in a way that would drive me into a chaotic state of panic. Instead, I danced, I cried, I listened, I felt all the feelings, I made new choices and knew that even those mornings when a dream or vision of the future came through me that didn't feel good, I had a choice to co-create with it or create a new story.

That is why I am here now—to help you co-create your own story. I want to reveal the biggest secret I know, that chaos might be on the TV, outside your door, or raging inside of you, but you have a choice. You have a choice in how you want to see it, dance with it, and take responsibility for it. You have a choice in how you want to feel, what you want to do, what you want to create, and who you want to be. We all have that power. We all have the field of all possibilities within ourselves, and you get to choose how it plays out.

Where do you begin? Within. It begins with having the courage to go within, to listen to the voice, listen to your body that is always conversing with you whether you are listening or not, it's speaking to you, your dreams are too, there are messages all around you and within you asking you questions. It just takes a little bit of practice to translate the messages and trust yourself to listen again.

So what questions are you being asked now? Do you have a sinking feeling at your job? Do you want to move somewhere new? Are you in a relationship that is not feeling aligned but you don't know why? Is something dreadful happening to you—like divorce, death of a loved one, or an illness—that might be an invitation to a new story? What messages are coming through in your body, your dreams, your feelings, your obsessive thoughts? Lean in and listen. It might be the best thing you ever co-create.

All those moments I saw coming, I didn't have control over other people's actions but I had the choice in how to respond to them. I have come to embrace that chaos is an act of creation, and I get to choose how I want to choreograph my life.

ABOUT THE AUTHOR
PHOEBE LEONA

Phoebe Leona is the founder of nOMad always at OM, which offers transformational experiences within and around the world. She is also the creator of Mvt109™ (a somatic movement practice) and co-founder of TRIBE, which brings the tools of yoga to the military. She has been featured at DailyOM, TEDx, on podcasts and nOMad's, *The Space in Between*, and will publish her first book in 2021. Phoebe guides transformation through movement and expanded awareness practices, so you feel empowered and committed to embodying who you are to develop a greater sense of belonging in this world. Phoebe believes our outer relationships, communities, and planet will be more holistically integrated if we are more connected to our bodies and our inner world, which could help solve the problems of our physical, mental, and emotional bodies. The mantra she lives is, "awareness is the transformation."

Website: *https://www.nomadalwaysatom.com*
Instagram: *https://www.instagram.com/phoebeleona.love*
Facebook group: *https://www.facebook.com/groups/762253688031528*

ROXY SEWELL

HER INNER LABYRINTH

I stand here today, as a woman reborn, covered with invisible scars. These scars tell my story. They hold my pain with the same reverence as they hold my joy. They are symbols of my wholeness. My story is one of transformation. Like most of this nature, mine is also a tale of becoming. It is a story in which the death of who I was led to becoming who I am today. I am who I am because I rose from my very own ashes. My death was the threshold for my rebirth.

All of this, my death and rebirth, occurred in the most potent way. Here is my story, or at least part of it:

The date was October 5, 2012, the time precisely 7:00 pm. It was a Friday night in Atlanta. I was twenty-five years old and I was getting married. The night was a crisp autumn night with the waning moon up above. There was not a raindrop in sight. It was one of those fall nights that lure you into stillness, allowing the veils between worlds to fade as time itself becomes stretchy and long. This was a magic moment...*my* magic moment. I stood there at the edge of the aisle, at the edge of my threshold, taking it all in.

These were my last moments as the version of myself that existed all those years before when I was a child, unmarried, and still wore the last name of my family—my maiden name. I knew that once the doors opened and I walked down the aisle, I would change...things would change. I wasn't ready.

With every breath I took, time slowed down just a little bit more, allowing me to continue standing there at the edge of a moment that exists right before everything shifts. My moment between moments. My breath between breaths. My space between phases. As I stood there, I allowed myself to stand still.

I began to take in the details of the moment, etching them into my very bones. I noticed my dad on my left, our elbows interlocked. He held me with nostalgic pride. I was his youngest daughter and the first to be married. We had dreamt of this walk my entire life. When I looked into his eyes, I was filled with memories of my childhood. Memories in which he and my mother wrapped their arms of love around my sister and me. The way in which my father loved my mother was a source of inspiration for me. Up until this moment, it was all I wanted, to be loved like her. The love my parents share is of mythic proportions.

They met in high school, my dad fell in love with my mother at first sight, my mother took a while to fall in love with my father. But once she did, she never let him go. Their marriage was imperfect and perfect all at once. Through every hardship, they leaned into one another and found solace in the person they had decided to share their life with. I admired them and aspired to have a love like theirs. I felt proud that I was standing at my threshold. I wondered if this was how my mother felt on her wedding day.

I soaked each of the memories from my childhood up, drank them up like nectar, and then shifted my eyes down to the soft flowers I was holding in my right hand. There, my mind began to wander, moving through the events that had unfolded throughout our engagement. The infidelity that was brought to my attention, the way I knew deep in my core that it had been happening long before I officially knew. The way I feared all that infidelity brought. The way it made me feel heartbroken and small all at once. I never told anyone about this. Why was I thinking about it now?

I took a big breath in, filling my lungs with the strength of my own soul. "Not tonight. Don't think about that tonight." And with that thought, I shifted my gaze to the diamond ring on my finger, remembering the night we got engaged. "Everything will change once we get married," I told myself. "Everything will change".

At my next breath, the doors in front of me opened. Pachelbel's Canon in D minor began to fill the room with music. I looked over at my dad and noticed the tears in his eyes. "Are you ready?" he asked me. "Yes," I replied. Time was still moving at the pace of the moon. Slow, stretched out, steady. I began my walk down the aisle, allowing my gaze to fall on three guests who were looking at me in awe from the pews. I saw my aunt and noticed her tears, I saw my cousin smiling at me, I saw my grandmother standing as the proud matriarch. And then, I saw him. I walked straight to him feeling all of my worries drift away. My dad placed my hand in his, kissed my cheek and walked away. Time began to move once again. I had crossed my threshold. I had moved from maiden to wife. I walked with the waning moon.

Looking back, I am in awe of how my October wedding was the embodiment of both the autumn season and the waning moon that held it. Both are symbols of transition. When the moon wanes, it moves from the light of the full moon into the darkness of the new moon. Similarly, when fall arrives, it moves from the light of summer into the darkness of winter. The ever-growing darkness, and the movement from light to dark, lures us into our inner worlds, allowing us to converse with ourselves and discover all things new. The Fall Equinox shortens our days and invites us to spend more time in the darkness while simultaneously stretching the night time and creating a longer space for contemplation. It is here, in this space, that mother nature shows us that nothing is permanent, that even the most sought-after summer blooms have an end. To end means to release. Both the autumn and the waning moon invite us to shed our past seasons and step into the unknown new. My wedding day was full of deep symbolism...symbolism I was unaware of. Perhaps if I had known, I could have seen what was coming. Or perhaps I wasn't supposed to see it back then.

My wedding was beautiful; my marriage, on the other hand, was as dark as the dark moon herself—both promising an ending, a death, and a new beginning that would only arise from the pain of transformation.

By the time 2015 came along, it felt as if my life was being held together by a single thread that was almost broken itself. The infidelity that loomed silently over my head on my wedding day became a tornado of endless affairs that ripped through our marriage. The more time we spent as husband and wife, the more we drifted away from one another. I began to resent him and myself for everything that was occurring. Everything shifted. Every part of us that was once gentle became rough. The words spoken, the tone of voice used to communicate, the sex that we had, the way humor was used—they became abusive normalcies. My world became a ticking time bomb. The floor I walked on was made of eggshells, and I somehow always knew exactly how to take the wrong step at just the right time.

Then, on July 11, 2015, two and half years after we became husband and wife, our marriage came to an end, ending our ten-year relationship.

My divorce was traumatic. It cracked me open into a million pieces, shattering me and leaving me as an empty, hollow corpse. Depression entered my life here. It wrapped itself around me like a weighted blanket, devouring me with its pressure. I was left numb and lifeless. My depression acted as a separator between my body and myself. The more I resisted, the denser and more suffocating it became. Until finally, I disappeared into a deep, dark space from which no one would be able to save me—no one, that is, except for me. This was the darkest time of my life. It was my death.

Both depression and divorce are often experienced in the hollow walls of loneliness. They initiate us into a ritual of death. Divorce is a death. It is the death of the life that was currently being lived. It is the death of the person who once existed. The version of myself who walked down that aisle and became a wife at twenty-five years old no longer existed. She no longer exists. She and her life disappeared in one single breath. My death came with an emptiness. An emptiness so hollow that it swallowed me whole. Who was I now? I had no idea. I had enmeshed myself with my ex-husband in such a way that when we ended as a couple, there was nothing left of me. And so, I disappeared. I became a living ghost. Depression met me here in my space of nothingness. Depression is another death. It is the darkness that strips us from ourselves. It forces us to walk in the space of in-between. A place where the dead do not fully die.

Healing is not linear. It is an ever-unfolding journey. It moves in the shape of a spiral or a labyrinth. It echoes the phases of the moon. Slowly weaving its way around and calling us into our pain, into our healing. Round and round we go, entering into ourselves and resurfacing only to re-enter again. This walk is hard and requires us to undergo many deaths in between. Shedding all of who we were in order to rise into all of who we are. This is our becoming.

Every experience of healing is a deeply personal one. Mine happened in a space that exists deep within myself. A space that I call my inner labyrinth. It is a place where I exist in my wholeness, as both my shadow and light. Every memory, every dream, every moment of my life is there deep within my core. The parts of myself that I hide away in the darkest corners of my soul, there I can find them, face them, lean into them and get to know myself on a deeper, more forgiving level. For me, I had to come face to face with the parts of myself that felt unworthy, not good enough, and unloved. I had to sit with my anger, my bitterness, my desire to no longer live. I had to hold these parts without judgement and with deep compassion. I had to show up for myself over and over again, allowing the journey to unfold without controlling it. During a time in which I felt myself disappear into nothing, the choice to see myself as something was a radical one.

One year after my divorce, I traveled to Thailand. On one early morning while the city was asleep, I rode my bike and heard a voice whisper a song into my ear, "Let go. Let go, sweet one", And so I did.

I let go of the version of me that existed with him. Shedding our dreams that never came to life.

A few moments later, I heard the voice whisper her sweet song again, "Let go some more. Let go of something that hurts". And so I did.

There, on that misty morning, I released the family that was no longer mine. I let go of his mother, the one I called "second mommy", I let go of loving her like a daughter. I let go of his father and the bond we shared. I let go of his younger brother, the one who came into my life at age nine and was now twenty years old. The one who I loved as if he were my own sibling. One by one, I saw their faces. One by one, I said goodbye, my tears falling down with the rain above. The earth Herself blessing my grief.

A few days later, while barefoot on the beach in Ko Phi Phi, I heard the voice whisper again, "Now, let go even more."

And so I did. There on the beach, I surrendered completely as I danced under the moonlight, crying and laughing both at the same time. "Perhaps I am a phoenix," I told myself, "Here I am, birthing myself from my very own ashes."

My healing journey became shrouded in ritual. The moon became my most intimate mentor. Her movement forever reminding me that we are shapeshifters capable of rebirthing ourselves from *nothing* into *everything*. My divorce and depression were my death. I had to mourn them, accept my new reality, and walk the underworld of my inner labyrinth to shed my past and birth my future. For so long, I thought I would not survive the journey. I feared I would stay lost forever—a ghost to the world above, a shadow in the world below. But I walked the phases of the moon, ritual by ritual, meditation through meditation. I kept showing up and moving with her. Deepening my relationship with her and, more importantly, with myself. Taking this journey inward allowed me to learn how to love myself and all of my story. Most importantly, it taught me to heal my trauma in my own sacred way and gave me permission to see both the beauty and the pain of it all.

Fast forward to the date October 5, 2020, exactly eight years after I walked down the aisle. On this date, I performed the most intimate ritual for myself. I held a funeral for the version of me that died all those years ago. I invited my dear friend Leah to join me. When she arrived, she immediately dropped into the energetic space I had created. In a silence as holy as the silence found deep in the woods or in a nurturing cave, Leah and I moved as if we were two parts of the same breath. Out in my front yard, we each grabbed a stick and began to dig a hole. We dug and dug until finally, we both stopped. I pulled out a tiny box, opened it, revealing the two items sitting inside: my old wedding ring and engagement ring. Closing my eyes and witnessing the bravery that lived inside me all those years ago when I was scared and brave all at once, I held the rings against my heart, silently thanked myself, and then placed them into the earth. With our bare hands, Leah and I then covered them with dirt.

I sat in this emotional space for a few weeks, waiting for the moon to turn into her darkness, leaving the world lightless. When this night came, I sat under the dark sky and wrote an obituary for my past self.

My obituary ended up reading like a love letter. I had spent so many years of my life hating that version of myself, thinking she was weak and resenting her for all the pain she brought. I hated her for getting married when she knew of his infidelity, for breaking apart when it all ended, for falling into her hole of depression, and for not walking away. But as I sat there on that dark night, I was filled with a remembrance of my own strength. I poured so much love and forgiveness into her. Thanking her for being brave. For walking down that aisle and for allowing herself to break into those million pieces all those years ago. She did not fear death; instead, she trusted herself to fall apart and to crack wide open. She did this so that she could break free from all that held her captive. From him, from her limiting beliefs, from her false sense of self. She was not weak; she was the bravest version of me.

Sometimes when we live in such darkness, the only way for the light to come in is through the cracks. Sometimes, we have to fall apart in order for us to make the journey back home to ourselves, back to wholeness, back to truth.

Once I finished writing, I read my obituary aloud, both to myself and the dark hidden moon. Then through my tears and through the fire, I burned it. One final offering. I took the ashes, dipped my fingers in them and drew a crescent moon on my forehead. Baptizing myself in my very own ashes. I no longer rejected "her". Instead, I walked forward and proudly integrated all of who she was into all of who I am. I am the new moon that was birthed from her darkness. I am because she was.

The most beautiful gift that my healing journey gave to me was the gift of an expanded heart. The more I stepped into myself, the more I fell in love with the totality of who I am and who I was becoming. As my heart grew in size, it began whispering to me, telling me that it was safe to love another. The man I fell in love with had been there through it all, watching me as I rose, honoring the depth of my journey.

Today I stand before you, a priestess with invisible scars. I will not heal you; I would never take away your sacred journey. I am here to hold space. To hold a light. To whisper back your truth. To invite you into ritual and to celebrate every single step with you. There is sacredness in pain, and that sacredness is you.

ABOUT THE AUTHOR
ROXY SEWELL

Roxy Sewell, MS is a reiki healer, yoga and meditation teacher, priestess, shadow worker, mystic, and mentor. She is unique as an energy healer in that she also holds an MS in Mental Health Counseling. Roxy is dedicated to helping others heal, alchemize their grief and wounds, and shed what no longer serves them to unapologetically step forward into their sovereignty. She believes that we all have the power to become our own healers. Her most sacred work is done by sitting with you, bearing witness to your journey, celebrating your rising, and holding space for all of who you are—both your shadow and your light. Roxy is the founder of Her Inner Labyrinth, LLC and the creator of 'An evening of myth and healing'—a goddess invoked and ritual-infused healing circle. Roxy lives in Atlanta, GA, with her husband and their two cats.

Website: www.herinnerlabyrinth.com
Instagram: https://www.instagram.com/roxy.sewell
Email: roxy@herinnerlabyrinth.com

SARAH COLLINS

THE ANSWER HAS ALWAYS BEEN YOU

Before I let the world tell me otherwise, I always knew I was surrounded by magic.

I still remember how it felt, laying on the grass in my front yard as a child, seeing stories unfold in the clouds that rolled by. I remember the day I climbed the tree in my backyard in the pouring rain and how I fell, staring up through the branches with the wind knocked out of me, realizing with deep reverence how the trunk of the tree had caught me. I remember how the full moon looked as I peered out of my bedroom window at night and how the hydrangea bush in my backyard smelled after rain. To me, the world was a place of endless wonder.

However, when Love runs through your bones in this way, it's easy to fall into questioning yourself in a society that prizes logic, achievement, and productivity. When this doubt starts to creep in, you become disconnected from the magical world that you once thought you could see so clearly. You start to believe that the lens everyone else is looking through must be the right one, and something must be wrong with the vivid, technicolor glasses you've been wearing since birth. After all, everyone around you seems to be on the same page, seeing and experiencing things in one way, so they must be right and you must be wrong, right?

Nope. Far from it, my love.

Trust me, I get it. I was there, too. For a long time, I let go of that magical world, and I locked it away. I now have so much compassion for that version of myself who was afraid and just wanted to be like everyone else.

I didn't realize, though, that doing this is, in fact, was what kept me in a cage.

It wasn't where I lived, it wasn't my relationship, and it wasn't my job (although these things shifted majorly as I began to follow my true heart).

It was me, constantly seeking outside of myself for the answers. It was putting my faith and trust in every corner of the Universe except within myself.

The process of unlearning this deeply ingrained habit of giving my power away has been a journey, to say the least. It has since taken me to depths and heights I could have never imagined for myself, every detour and off-road leading me back home to myself, and my own inner wisdom, time and time again.

So, come—lay in the grass with me, put your bare feet on the Earth, and let me share with you the story of how I set myself and my sacred heart free.

About a year before this moment, I took a terrifying leap of faith that catapulted me onto my spiritual path. I was working in psychology research at the time and living in Denver with my partner of nearly six years. We shared a beautiful apartment and the sweetest, most loving dog. Life was pretty normal—going to work from nine to five, ending the day with Netflix, and spending our weekends finding new hikes and hanging out at the local breweries. There was nothing overtly wrong with it. In fact, it was filled with sweetness in so many ways, and I loved my partner and our life together very much.

And yet, something in my soul was restless.

It showed up every so often and would keep me up at night. *Is this really all there is?* I would wonder, timid at the seemingly insurmountable largeness of the question and terrified of what could lie beneath it. I could feel my heart calling out for something, but I couldn't for the life of me figure out what it was.

I would then immediately push the thoughts down, shaming and calling myself ungrateful for letting myself go there. I rationalized the feelings back into their box, re-explaining to my heart for what seemed like the millionth time that we were, indeed, happy and that any thought trying to tell me otherwise was just anxiety. And still, months later, they would crawl back into my consciousness, and I would lay awake, wondering if I would feel this lost forever.

Looking for some relief from this storm growing inside me, I started to peek my head into spirituality. I found myself gravitating toward astrology, reading about manifestation and practicing yoga at a sweet little studio called Karma. I had befriended the owners of the studio and started cleaning it once a week in exchange for classes. This space became my safe haven—a quiet corner of the universe where I could let my soul light begin to unfold before my rather curious eyes. The two hours I spent alone in that studio were sacred, and ultimately where I rediscovered the magic within me that had been tucked away since childhood. I wandered and twirled about, cleaning as I went, pulling oracle cards and letting my imagination float into the abyss as I scanned the pages of books in the meditation room.

This newness brought so much joy and light to my life. It was so beautiful to witness. And yet, as this magic began to grow, so too did that familiar restlessness in the pit of my stomach. There was a voice coming from deep within my soul, and I could no longer drown it out with logic and positive thinking. What once was a low rumbling became loud and confronting, coming through to me in dreams and in the distance growing between my partner and me. It came in the dissatisfaction I felt in my job and that old familiar question, now hitting a fever pitch: *Is this really all there is?*

On a Wednesday afternoon in February, the doubts about my relationship started to creep their way back into my heart. At this point, I knew I couldn't push them down any longer. My soul was speaking and I needed to listen. I finally asked the Universe in a moment of desperation, "Is this just going to keep happening until I leave?!"

And to my shock, a loud but gentle voice rang through my mind, clear as day: "Yes."

So, after blood-curdling screaming and wailing and yelling at the Universe about how I didn't want to and that I could never possibly do that,

That's exactly what I did.

In true Gemini fashion, I danced between the crashing waves of oceanic grief, and the vibrant light of freedom that I could sense was slowly steeping into my bones. I was terrified and joyful at the possibilities of what was to come. For the first time in my life, I had absolutely no clue what I would do next. All I could see were my two feet in front of me, taking one step after another. Despite not being used to the whole concept of "trust and surrender", I leaned into it with my whole being, reminding myself of what I had recently learned—that the Universe always has our back, and that big leaps of faith are held and supported beyond what we can possibly conceive of.

I quickly manifested a little apartment in downtown Denver, a short drive from where I lived, with the sweetest new roommate. It was in the sweetness and tranquility of this space that I truly began to find myself again—a process that led me to realize just how much of me had left.

The first aspect of myself that came to greet me was my Inner Child. In this space of newness and play, joy filled my heart and lungs as I traded in the climbing gear my partner had bought me for bare feet and water coloring outside. I rediscovered my childhood love of Ireland and started studying ancient Celtic practices. I baked brownies in my underwear and planted wildflower seeds and sang to the stars. The world was my oyster in my own sacred unfolding.

And yet, I soon discovered that within my Inner Child came another aspect of myself that was ready and asking to be seen.

My Shadow.

For those of you who are new to the path, the Shadow refers to the parts of ourselves that we prefer not to look at or deal with—and yet, these are the parts that need our love most. Within them lies the root of what we came here to learn from, heal and ultimately let go of. I have learned to love my Shadow deeply, as I now know she is the sacred carrier of my unique gifts and my soul's medicine—but I didn't always feel this way. I spent a long time running from her, judging her as the source of everything "wrong" with me.

As it turns out, the more you run from your Shadow, the more it will make itself known.

My Shadow first manifested in a way best described through the archetype of the Wounded Maiden. The wounded maiden distrusts herself and her intuition, often leaning heavily into logic and always putting others on pedestals. She feels insecure and unsafe within, so she seeks the answers to life's questions outside of herself. She looks to others for what to do, say and be, thinking that safety and love will come with fitting in and being accepted.

If I could describe myself from late childhood until one year ago, it would be this description to a tee.

When I was young, I felt extremely different from everyone around me. I was diagnosed with epilepsy when I was five years old. In a well-meaning effort to protect me, my parents wanted me to feel like I was just another normal kid. We didn't talk about it at all. One would only notice it if they looked in the shadows. The fact that I wet the bed until well into elementary school. The horse-sized pills I took with my applesauce at night. The whispers between parents before a sleepover and the conferences with teachers before the start of every school year. It felt so shrouded in shame that it became easier to pretend it wasn't there at all.

On top of that, my traits weren't the ones celebrated in mainstream culture. I was a daydreamer, lost in her own world of princesses, magic, adventure and far off kingdoms. I preferred climbing trees and playing in nature to sports, and I didn't do overwhelmingly well in school because I didn't feel connected to what

I was learning. I was emotional, feeling in oceanic depths and firestorms that left anyone in my path perplexed or terrified.

Experiencing life in this way often left me feeling alone and like something was wrong with me. I didn't realize that the exact things that made me feel different were, in fact, my intuitive abilities and gifts, shrouded by logical explanations and misunderstanding. It wasn't until recently that I began to understand just how deeply intuitive and empathic I was and that the worlds of my own creation were indeed very real.

Over time, I started to disconnect from myself and the magical world within me, looking to the external world for relief from the pain and dissonance of feeling different. I wanted more than anything to feel like I belonged somewhere. I found a way to shape-shift myself in every crowd—morphing myself to the version that I knew would be accepted, received and approved of. Fitting in became my method of survival. I believed that if I could master being what everyone else wanted me to be, I would be safe, happy, and loved.

This pattern slowly began to solidify itself, following me into my adult life in the form of people-pleasing and seeking the answers to all of life's questions outside of myself. I got so used to believing that I needed to be fixed that I doubted all of my thoughts, feelings, and perceptions. I would write myself off as "too emotional". Every perception I had about myself and others was judged and shamed in a ritual response of self-gas-lighting. I believed that simply because these thoughts and feelings came from me meant that they must be wrong, and someone else needed to tell me what was right.

When my awakening came, and I was fully immersed in my spiritual path, I was so eager for someone to tell me exactly what to do to activate my gifts and live out my purpose. All I wanted was for someone out there to confidently tell me what was true and what wasn't, and what was right for me and what wasn't, so that I could finally "fix myself" and be a "Good Spiritual Person".

The universe responded to this by hand-delivering every lesson it could muster to show me, clear-as-day, what I was doing to myself by giving my sacred power away so willingly to anyone that came along. It gave me every opportunity under the sun to realize that the gifts I was so desperately seeking were in the very place I was denying the most—myself. My true heart and the magical kingdom that was my soul, deep within my being, that I had abandoned so long ago.

The lessons came in the form of new relationships, where I turned a blind eye to the old, cage-like patterns of co-dependency that were resurfacing. They came in the form of the earth-shattering heartbreak and loss of community that followed.

They came in the form of coaches who manipulated my pain points, and in constantly buying into what they told me over my own intuition.

They came in the form of tirelessly asking everyone around me what my purpose was, and in the frustration and helplessness I felt as I went around in circles, waiting wild-eyed and desperate for a sign.

They came in the lightning strike moment when I realized that I hadn't had epilepsy at all, but rather a sacred gift of visioning. They came in the grief that poured through me as I mourned my lifelong pattern of self-doubt and self-betrayal that stemmed from a diagnosis that never even belonged to me.

The Universe looked on each time, patient and loving, as I gave my power away—waiting for me to finally notice what I was doing to myself. Time and time again, I would tell myself that my perceptions and tidal waves of emotion were "just me being judgmental" or that it was my "ego resistance", and I would free-fall into a painful, heart-wrenching karmic lesson.

I walked through this countless times in the past year, each time my life shifting drastically, trying to position itself in such a way that I could see what was happening.

It finally all hit the fan, and I found myself on my own once again, able only to see my two feet in front of me.

This sacred pause, a true cosmic void, is when I finally surrendered to the call within. I slowed down, turned in toward my own heart, and said, "Okay. I'm here. And I'm listening."

Now, you'll never catch me saying that all of this happened TO me because I deeply believe in both free will and that everything we walk through is exactly what we call in for our highest good. We can also only experience in our reality that which, to some degree, exists within ourselves. We learn at times through painful contrast and always what our soul needs to grow and expand in Love. When we alchemize these experiences into powerful, transformative, embodied wisdom, they become our sacred medicine—the healing gifts we were meant to share with this world.

I don't tell you all of this so that you shut the blinds and run away from the world in fear and distrust. Far from it. In fact, if I could give you one piece of advice, it would be to run into this world with your heart leading the way and your mind wide open. But do so from a space of knowing and valuing who YOU are. Seek guidance not from those who claim to have all the answers, but from those who lead you back to yourself.

Not the person your parents wanted you to be. Not the version that society says you should be.

You.

Because your channel is sacred, and your truth matters far beyond what you can even comprehend. Your thoughts, feelings, perceptions, and ideas are your sacred guides, leading you into your own soul's liberation. You came here with a mission on your heart that only you could see through, and this world needs you now more than ever.

Learning how to do this for myself—to truly listen within and trust that guidance—is what set me free.

It's what led me to start my business, supporting other womxn in alchemizing their own inner child and activating their sacred gifts.

It's what led me to reclaim my identity as a Healer, confidently sharing my herbal medicine and magic with the world.

It's what led me to stand in my power and speak my truth, even when the whole world seemed against me.

It's what led me to California and living by the ocean, rapidly manifesting my dream life that just one year ago seemed impossible.

It's what continues to lead me back home to myself again, every time.

So, beautiful soul reading this, know that everything and anything is possible. When you trust yourself and leap, you will be caught in the arms of the Universe every time.

So, go ahead. Claim your divinity. Step boldly into this world. Hold onto your heart and let it guide you the whole way. Surrender the rest.

Because the answer has been you, all along.

ABOUT THE AUTHOR
SARAH COLLINS

Sarah Collins is an Inner Child alchemist, intuitive herbalist and the founder of Sunlight Speaks. She is passionate about empowering and guiding her clients in their own beautiful unfolding story. She embodies the teaching that the spaces within us that we resist the most are the key to unlocking a life of pure joy, passion, and liberation. In addition to her work as a guide, she has an Etsy shop featuring her handcrafted herbal healing products that facilitate deeper levels of self-connection. Her work is a true testament to the transformational power of coming home to the wisdom of the Earth and learning to accept, witness, and deeply love all parts of the self. Her medicine is one of radical authenticity, compassion, gentleness, and diving deep. She resides in San Diego, California, where she enjoys connecting with the plants, deepening her intuitive practices, and playing in community.

Linktree: https://linktr.ee/sunlightspeaks
Facebook: https://www.facebook.com/Sunlight-Speaks-107177324917290
Email: sarah.et.collins@gmail.com
Etsy: https://www.etsy.com/shop/SunlightSpeaks?ref=seller-platform-mcnav
Instagram: https://www.instagram.com/sunlightspeaks

STACY JOHNSTON

UNDERNEATH THE MUSIC

Life has a rhythm. A song to sing and a dance to perform. We are life. One day, the Grand Overall Designer looked around and decided the world needed one of You. At that moment, you were gifted with a story to write, a song to sing, and a dance to dance. This story is your legacy, its words and wisdom becoming the lyrics to your song. And then you dance. Your faith and choices, circumstances, honor and fear, laughter, courage, joy and pain are all instruments in the orchestra of your life. You choose along the way to merely dance to the music, left to its own devices, the consequences deciding your beat. Or, by grace and acceptance, with courage and integrity, you can choose to be the conductor of your own symphony and the choreographer of your dance. After all, it's your song. It's your dance. Sing the song. Dance the dance. Take the final bow.

All too often, culture and environment teach us to exist within the norm, "Please, in the box you go," and we comply. It starts slowly and without much notice. Not by any direct fault or weakness, we allow our family, spouse or partner, children, career and economic status, and even our social media standing, to write our story for us. In time, and with our unspoken permission, they begin to orchestrate our song and control our beat. We get up in the morning, dress in the costume placed neatly on the bed, and dance the dance they have chosen. Time passes, and we hardly notice that we are giving up our best steps up to someone else to perform.

In a single moment along the way of your everyone-else-planned-journey, a strange feeling begins to creep in, almost like an annoying noise in the back of your hearing. That flying insect you know you can hear but cannot find. It is all static and flashes at first. Sound by sound, it begins to come in clearer. Is that a song I'm hearing? You can't pick out the beat and the words sound confused. Maybe it is uncomfortable, like too much noise. Maybe it is too faint. Where is the Power? And what is up with that beat? You realize you can't possibly dance to the song filling your head. Suddenly, you begin to realize it is the song you are playing to the world. And the shift begins. It is time to change the music.

I grew up as a dancer. My mom was a dance teacher, my father loved to dance, and we were solid DMA (Dance Masters of America) members. My entire young life was filled with recitals and costumes, competitions, rehearsals, and music. Lots and lots of music. Throughout my dance experience, I always had a deep respect for the arts, the beauty of Ballet, and the safe freedom it provides for your soul. Alas, I am a tap dancer at heart. I love the energy and the rhythm of tap. If executed well, it creates a song of its own. As a young girl learning the art of tap, my mom would say, "To be the best tap dancer, you cannot dance to the music because the music changes. It rises and falls, builds and fades. If you will listen closely, underneath the music, there is one sound. Maybe it is a drum, or possibly a single guitar note. This sounds' only job it is to keep everything else on time. It manages the rhythm. That is your dance partner. That one constant, true sound underneath." I tapped for over forty years with a love and a passion for the rhythm. Little did I know that one day this simple but critical lesson on the art of tap dancing that I passed on to my own students would change the trajectory of my life.

For me, it was the day I was done. I was tired, scared, confused and disillusioned with life itself. I just didn't get it. I had a great husband, three healthy, amazing kids, a strong and true faith, and a thriving dance studio business. We danced. We roped and rode bulls. I taught Sunday school and bible school. I volunteered, planned events, ran 4-H projects and held Cowboy Church in my living room. I was room mom, team mom, dance mom and rodeo mom. Still, something vital was missing. Me. One beautiful, awful day, I finally pulled my car over to the side of the road to have a 'Come to Jesus' meeting with the Big Man Himself. Why was I surrounded by blessings and feeling like I was watching it all from the outside? Where was the disconnect? As I cried and prayed and yelled and prayed some more, a new sound began to enter my awareness. It was strange yet familiar, still missing something that would have kept it all together. Suddenly I realized it was the same thing I was missing. That one constant, true sound underneath. Rhythm. The song had lost its rhythm and I had lost the rhythm of ME.

Like fog beginning to lift on a warm, muggy morning, my mind began to clear and almost explode with a new understanding. All my years of training were about more than knowing the steps and smiling on cue. They were a preparation for life. Something deep inside me switched to dancer mode, and I began to think of the magic of the music, the story and the dance. To perform your dance is have overcome the rigors of time, energy, tears, sweat, joy and frustration to take that final bow. I needed my song back. My soul needed to dance again. This time around, it needed to be my dance.

As I began to walk this new journey of self-love and discovery, I had to find a safe space in my head and heart. I went to the safest place I knew. I went to dance class. In the mirrored walls that held no secrets, the judgment was my own. In my mind, it was like designing an entire performance to one song. My song. It built and faded, the tempo rising and falling, the cadence changing and circling but staying the same underneath. Positive affirmation and self-forgiveness became my daily warm-up and opening to new insight. Gratitude and self-grace, my wind down and bow. As those practices became new habits, I was able to choreograph my own dance with a belief in myself I thought long gone. The best way to explain it is to invite you to dance class. So, join me, if you please, on a dancer's journey to rediscover my dance partner underneath the music.

The first thing I needed to rediscover on this adventure was the rhythm of me. Rhythm is primal, unbiased and neutral. It is non-judgmental and universal. Underneath the suit, the dress, the sweats, the roles, the duties and the expectations exists the authentic rhythm of you. This is the "You" that has a favorite color and a favorite cartoon. This "You" knows how you like your eggs and how you feel about love and success and rejection. Somewhere along the way, I had forgotten that "You" matters and "You" needed to be on the calendar. I had programmed myself to believe that it is selfish to practice good 'me-care', to spend any time focusing on growing and attending to myself. A not-so-quiet voice began to ask, "What makes the masses more worthy than you?" Then, it was, "Why walk this journey with a half-written song and a dance with no bow?" In my soul, I knew I wanted a dance with a sweeping, majestic, final bow, not a chorus line curtsey. I wanted my life to matter.

When I finally began to believe in my song and the dance steps became more familiar, I had to re-discover my rhythm and not get lost in the music again. In our world and society at large, there is a lot of chatter and static on the station. There are a whole lot of people wanting to sing their song. I had to become very aware of *whose* song I listened to. I wanted to hear my own. So, how do you tune out the noise and hear your song? You rediscover *your* song through and through then, you sing it, that's how. You show up strong and you live out loud.

Feeling ready again to show up strong, back to mental dance class I went. The lesson I was seeking was there. Long ago I had learned that to execute a flawless tap routing, you must remember that the environment around you can be noisy and congested. You cannot hear your rhythm in the place the noise will take you. You must listen underneath in a place that the one true sound is the loudest. So I prayed. As I began to rediscover what the rhythm was about for me, the lens through which I was viewing life began to shift like a turn in a kaleidoscope. As I began to change the way I saw things, what I saw began to change. I saw the rhythm of me. And a new, inviting light began to shine through the pieces of colored glass. This glow provided light to the next piece of the dance.

The second element underneath the perfect tap song is tempo. It is the integrity of the song. Even though the rhythm changes and the cadence can travel up or down, the tempo is in the basic creation of the song. Without integrity and a defined tempo, the rest is in vain and no one dances to the song. It is the same for us. If you are a person of integrity, it shows up in your relationships, business, home, and everyday life. It is the one part of you that should be unwavering and constant. It shapes the story of your legacy. Your integrity decides what is said about you after you leave the room and it is the story your grandchildren tell about you by what they carry forward. Integrity, like character, is not built in a crisis; it just shows up. I had decided to show up strong and live out loud. How? One step at a time. What was my true tempo? I realized I needed to take a good hard look at who I was showing up as and ask myself the tough questions like, "If I met me, would I like me?" and "Am I showing up to be the best spouse, partner, parent, friend, teacher, coach or mentor I can be?" Like a dancer in front of the secret-free mirror, it was time to learn about me.

I began to pray and seek true love, respect and understanding of my authentic self again—the barefoot me with no dance shoes. I realized how easy it had become to step into the shoes of mom, wife, daughter, sister, teacher, volunteer or friend. I had almost forgotten what sweet grass on a warm summer day felt like between the toes of my soul. To dance to the tempo of me. Learning to re-love myself was a challenge. Loving your authentic self requires ownership, forgiveness, grace and recognition that you were crafted perfectly flawed by design. I found it much easier to extend those gifts to others than to grant space for them to myself.

This new dance I was working on perfecting had a sound rhythm and the tempo was coming into check, but the spin and circle, fly and dive of the cadence of my life were still out of my control. I needed understanding. Why did I believe that coincidence happened on purpose? That it is all a big circle covered with the pieces of our cross. I began to ask for insight and wisdom to see who I had become and why. I needed to own the consistency in the chaos of my own cadence. So, He showed me the circle dance.

Do you remember that mean girl in high school? You know the one. She built a club of hate girls that haunted you in the halls, embarrassed you at every opportunity, taunted you in public and maybe even chased you with her car. Can you picture her now? That "mean girl" was me at sixteen. I wasn't mean to everyone. Just to that one new girl that decided she wanted to go out with my boyfriend. I was so mean to her that she ended up leaving the high school and I ended up in juvenile court. Through my sixteen-year-old lens, I was justified because she was the outsider. She started it. I just ended it. And now she was gone. As penitence for my bad behavior, I got a customary "I don't want to see you in my court again" slap on the hand. I counted it a victory. Over time, it left my mind and hid in my heart.

That absence of thought remained until the first day my oldest child came home from school, the victim of a bully. Well, I can tell you that every super defensive, How Dare You, Who is your Momma and Where's your momma thought I could have ever had came alive instantly. After the dust settled, so did my conscience and my heart. For the first time in over ten years, I thought about that girl I had bullied so relentlessly. Two things happened to me that day. First, I asked God to forgive me for what I had done to her, for who I had been just then and to remove any of that meanness that was left inside of me. Second, I hoped that maybe one day there would present an opportunity for me to right that wrong. That day, I traded my victory for regret and became a staunch advocate for kindness. Mean people suck.

Now jump ahead with me twenty-nine years from that day to this day. I am a family services specialist. In my care was a twelve-year-old boy with a brain condition called Cerebral Dysrythmia. His mom, blind since birth, and his retired veteran dad spent a great deal of their time managing both the symptoms and the resulting behavior of his condition. One morning, his mom went to wake him up for school only to discover that he had died of an aneurism in his sleep. While wanting to keep in tune with what he loved—Ninja turtles and everything green—they realized they could not afford to buy the green coffin.

A few phone calls later and with the help of an amazing friend, a Go-Fund-Me page was established to meet the cost. In just days, the coffin was paid for and they buried their son. A few days later, I was at the family's house, helping his mom go through the list of the cards and notes. We were working on writing 'Thank You' notes, and we came across the card for the coffin. No one recognized the name. It had come from half the country away, but they were intrigued and really wanted to reach out and send a special note of thanks. I never thought I'd say this but praise God for Facebook because we had our answer in just a few short minutes. The woman that purchased the coffin was... Yep, you guessed it... It was the girl that I had bullied all those years before. On my computer screen was the answer to a prayer I had prayed twenty-nine years ago. Challenge accepted. I was asking the questions. Who was I today? How much of what I had spent my entire adult life doing was tied to this experience? Was I still that same mean girl, or had I come to a place in my journey where I would embrace the opportunity, walk through the door and finally right that wrong? How about that integrity I was working on?

I called her. As only fate would have it, she and her family would be traveling toward me in just a few weeks. We scheduled to meet. I apologize profusely and repeatedly, working hard to justify my behavior. When it was her turn, she told me that she had forgiven me years before when she realized how strong the entire experience had made her. It had silently directed twenty-nine years of my life. I finally traded my regret for self-forgiveness.

Finally, the circle made sense. My cadence could spin. The rhythm and tempo finally in sync. It all sounded beautifully familiar, and my soul danced. I had found my dance partner again. I finally realized that I was not selfish to grow and love me. In fact, it was more selfish not to. I would cheat the world and myself out of the best me possible. I also understood that my growth would make some around me uncomfortable, like being at the wrong party. I would show up strong and dance my dance. They could choose to dance or not, but I choreograph the steps this time around.

What does it all mean, this journey underneath the music? It is the Magic of You. Although we cannot go back and make a new beginning, we can write a different ending. We are often led to believe that our past choices and mistakes have already written our story for us. This is the only song we get to sing. You are dancing your dance. Oh no! I beg to differ. Your journey does not define you; it merely designs you. It is YOUR choice. Underneath the music lies Your rhythm, the tempo of your integrity and the solid cadence of your faith. Show up strong, write the story, sing the song, dance the dance. Then, bow.

ABOUT THE AUTHOR
STACY JOHNSTON

    Stacy Johnston owns and operates Enlighten Up, a personal consulting firm based in Texas. Stacy is an internationally certified personal development coach and consultant, speaker, and trainer. Stacy spends her time guiding individuals, families, companies and communities to recognize the power of their influence and the importance of the legacy they leave behind. Her focus is to illuminate the magic of You. Stacy grew up in a dance studio family and was blessed to enjoy the beautiful world of the arts all of her life. Stacy is thirty-seven years married to a wonderful man with whom she has three children and six grandchildren. Stacy owned and operated Applause School of Dance for thirty years, took a pivot, and spent eleven years in the adolescent/adult substance abuse and mental health profession as a family services specialist. Her new joy running Enlighten Up and co-hosting two podcasts, *Un-Caped Heroes* and *Mid-Week Mind Candy*.

    You can connect with Stacy at:
https://www.facebook.com/stacyo.johnston or *enlightenup.stacyj@gmail.com*

    For podcast information reach out to:
herobuilder2020@gmail.com

SUZANNE WING

THE JOURNEY TO LIVING WILDLY PEACEFUL

Have you ever been skinny-dipping? There's an exhilaration that comes with running naked through the moonlight right before you jump in the water, followed by a feeling of serenity. The water supports you as you let go and simply float. That's how I wake up feeling most mornings—wildly peaceful.

It wasn't always like this. There was a time when my alarm would go off and a sense of dread would fall over my entire being. Everything seemed fine on the outside. On the inside, my physical, mental and spiritual health were crumbling. I couldn't shake the feeling of disorientation and disconnection. My mind, body and soul seemed separate from each other. Doctors had no answers for me. I tried supplements, diets and exercise. Despite the many changes I was making, my hair was still falling out, I had nightmares of wild animals trampling my home, and my memory was fading. My relationships—including my marriage—were not much more than surface-level conversations in passing. I was putting whatever energy I had toward taking care of my kids, but I didn't believe it was enough. Nothing I was doing was enough; I was an empty shell.

Something had to give. Something massive had to change. My husband and I discussed the disappointment with our relationship many times with no resolve. There was an endless loop of minuscule discrepancies that triggered traumatic outbursts of violent behavior, followed by months of quiet. Years of living with the uncomfortable feeling of tiptoeing around eggshells were taking their toll. I had reached the end of my ability to cope. On this particular day, I felt the tension rising, but thankfully, I had an excuse to get out of the house—my son had band practice and was waiting in the car, ready to go. And there it was, a ruckus in the garage. It was loud. I thought there must have been an accident, something falling, perhaps, but no, I opened the door to the garage, and there was my son in the car witnessing his father kick an old bench across the garage, shattering it into pieces. Disappointment and disgust took me over. I grabbed my purse and got in the car. As my husband began to walk into the house, he stopped, turned, picked up a bike pump and threw it as hard as he could...CRACK, my windshield spiderwebbed. CRACK, CRUNCH, SIZZLE. That was the sound it made, but the sound I heard was a strident, clear voice: "Next time, it's your face". Was it the voice of God, my guide, my soul? It didn't matter. It penetrated every cell in my body. I knew this was the final red flag, and this time, I was not going to hide it. I would not use it to wipe away my tears, as I have done too many times before. I grabbed my kids and went to a hotel. I took pen to paper and began to write the things I couldn't speak. Some of it was emotional gunk and some was pure fact. The rose-colored glasses that disguised the red flags were shattered with my windshield, leaving me with fragments of truth to piece together. I wish I could say that was the day I put it all back together and stepped fully into my power. The process of divorce is a painful game of blame and shame. Untangling a twenty-five-year relationship would only further contribute to my confusion and identity crisis. The wound that resulted from years of cumulative buried emotions was now open, raw and oozing. I was experiencing grief. I was grieving the life I planned and the life I thought I wanted. I was swimming in fear and self-doubt. I was in a tailspin to rock bottom.

I already had a list of failed attempts to recover my former sense of self. There were many efforts to achieve body-brain coherence. Therapy and lifestyle changes made incremental improvements and were necessary steps. But where was my passion, drive and desire for life? I had it once before, and I wanted it back more than anything else in the world. My attempts to reconnect with my old passions only fed nostalgia. I tried to cultivate the excitement I once had for my career as a designer, but years of staying at home to care for my family left me with an obsolete status in the professional world. Although I tried, I couldn't ignite that fire. I went from job to job to find some sort of spark. Maybe my job is just a job and not my purpose or passion.

I started gardening. This was the thing that got me out of my head and into my body. My nervous system was rebooting—connecting with the earth at a primal level is truly powerful. Digging in the dirt, pulling weeds, planting seeds, nurturing the plants, and collecting the harvest. I needed this physical work to center myself in my own body before I would be able to hear my own intuition. I experienced being intuitive and remembering past lives as a young person. Of course, I talked myself out of those ideas to blend in more easily with my community. Feeling the sting of rejection in my youth encouraged me to follow the herd and keep my esoteric interests a quiet pursuit.

After all those years of talking myself out of my own inner knowing, I was on a mission to recover it. I was seeking the feeling of wholeness. I wanted to hear my own guidance and be able to trust myself again. I could feel my soul calling to me from the other side of old beliefs and ideas that had been placed there by society to keep from expanding and becoming powerful. Being accepted by society and being accepted by my soul seemed contrary to each other. The call from my higher self was getting louder and louder. But the harsh reality on earth was also calling me loudly. Once again, I found myself between jobs and feeling trapped by life's conditions. I was restless and unable to identify the invisible wall that held me back. After all, I am now divorced; aren't I already free? I felt like a sinking ship. I started to lose hope and distracted myself with media binging—my drug of choice—when I came across a documentary about Ayahuasca and Shamanic journeying. I am not usually impulsive, but I responded to this like I was being called to dinner. I was hungry and it was time.

Within a few weeks, I was on a plane to Costa Rica. During the welcome ceremony, we were told that we were all part of a soul family and were all lightworkers. I felt more like a shadow dweller than a lightworker. I was ready to move out of the dark, and ayahuasca had a good reputation for creating permanent life changes. I was willing to do just about anything to feel whole and remember my passion for life, my love of nature and the earth, to remember my purpose for being here now. The shaman taught us how to work with medicine. We were told that Mother Ayahuasca would show us what we needed to heal the most to heal our hearts, call back our soul fragments and merge into wholeness. We were to not fight the process but try to understand why she brought the experience to us. My plant medicine journeys were filled with past life healing. I understood the origin of the fears I carried that were unrelated to my current life. I was shown places where I left tiny fragments of my soul in other lives, and they were called back to my original essence. Forgiveness of my offenders and myself in all lifetimes was imperative for the merging of the fragments.

The most challenging journey revealed the most stubborn aspect of my ego—the block I was trying to break down. In this journey, Mother Aya lovingly caressed me and gently sank my body deep into the earth. She was ready to serve up some tough love as she delivered me straight into Hell. I found myself chained to a cave wall while demons swirled around, singing different songs off key. Loud low gurgling in one ear and high pitch squeals in the other. I felt so sick but couldn't throw up. I started to laugh out loud and the grip released. The laughter coming from my mouth sounded evil. I didn't want the others in the room to think I was a witch. So, I stopped laughing and the grip resumed. This happened several times. I thought to myself, *I can't believe you came to the most beautiful place in the world to sit in Hell.* I started to laugh at myself and the grip released. Again, I sounded like a witch and stopped myself from cackling. Each time I stopped laughing, the grip brought me deeper into hell. It became increasingly horrifying. This pattern continued. Feeling anxious, trapped, nauseous, unable to expel the emotions. I was recalling what was taught by the shaman: to be freed from an unpleasant Ayahuasca experience, you have to understand the lesson or face the fear. I was cycling through the possible meanings, frantically trying to piece them together. Was I evil? Was this my karma? Had I lived a life in hell? Oh! I burst into real wholehearted laughter, and the entire Hell disappeared. The answer is *yes!* In this life! Staying in my marriage was a secret Hell, but I kept myself there because I was worried that other people would think I was an evil witch if I left.

I thought I was a free spirit—someone who had their own ideas and creative expression. The one thing I thought to be true about myself was a lie. Not only was I not a free spirit, I was trapped by my own doing. I was willing to stay trapped to avoid judgment and rejection. I let my need for societal and familial approval hold me and my children in a toxic environment. All my soul wants is for me to live and be the whole of who I am regardless of judgment. To honor my understanding of intuition, dreams, past lives and soul contracts without caring that I may upset someone. My soul left me with the task of proving that I will never doubt my own knowing ever again. That's the condition my soul gave me for living a whole life. Although, proving it meant I would be tested. I left Costa Rica ready to integrate this new in-depth understanding and agreement with my soul.

I knew I would devote myself to a spiritual path, but I wasn't sure how or in what way. In the meantime, I needed income and immediate change. I already had a job interview lined up. Everything about this job excited me, except the pay. I knew my budget was as streamlined as I could make it, and the math wasn't adding up. I also trusted the Universe to give me a sign, and I trusted my intuition to guide me. I jumped in the car and headed to the interview with a burst of enthusiasm. On the way there, I gave myself the usual pre-job interview pep talk. While I was doing my best to pump up my ego, I looked up to see a sign blocking the road— "DETOUR". I got chills. Wow, a literal sign. I was done with detours on my path. I knew something better lay ahead.

One week of transformation work wasn't going to create all the change I needed. The Universe brought more upheaval, which surprisingly left me the resources and time to continue my transformation. The next step brought me to journeys with Quantum Healing Hypnosis Technique℠, a method created by Delores Cannon, known for her past life regression work around the world. I was well versed with her work and life story. This was a natural progression, a much kinder approach to soul connections and past life regressions than Ayahuasca ceremonies. No international traveling, nausea or vomiting required.

I learned more about hypnosis and started training. I received and facilitated profound sessions that forever changed me. QHHT was only the beginning of my training and certifications in energy healings and various methods of hypnosis and regression therapy. I honored every call that came up from my core, and the Universe backed me. The more sessions I received and facilitated, the more easily I could complete my own journey of forgiveness and finally jump off the wheel of karma for good. My intuition is now fully intact and activated. I fully understand my purpose is to continue my own expansion and facilitate the expansion of others. Feeling passionate and following inspiration again was where the real healing happened. My clients find me when they are really ready to change at all costs. When they are ready to connect to their souls and commit to their path. When they are ready to repair the origin of the problems they're facing. When they are ready to retrieve trapped soul fragments. When Starseeds are ready to receive downloads and activations. When the earthbound are ready to get free from karmic contracts. When they are ready to be free from living in the trap of trauma. Helping people to dissolve the resistance that holds them from the freedom to live the most magical fulfilling life is wildly peaceful. That's how I wake up feeling most mornings—wildly peaceful.

ABOUT THE AUTHOR
SUZANNE WING

    Suzanne Wing is a spiritual hypnosis practitioner specializing in regression therapy. She helps clients break out of feeling stuck, resentful and powerless. She is able to free them from constraints by showing them why, when, where and how those constraints originated. While her work is spirit-based, she honors the framework of each client's belief system. She is also a Reiki practitioner and facilitates group workshops and offers DIY courses on the alchemy of transmutation, integration and how to channel your soul for guidance. She is also a channel for creativity and divination. She is trained in Delores Cannon's Quantum Healing Hypnosis Technique℠ (QHHT®), Introspective Hypnosis®, Soul Empowered Hypnosis® as well as classical and intuitive methods.

    If you want to reconnect with your inner magic and remember your power, please visit *http://www.QuantumJourney.co* or connect with her on *Facebook* (*https://www.facebook.com/HigherSelfHypnosis/*) and *Instagram* (*https://www.instagram.com/quantum_journeys/*).

VANESSA PARRADO

YOU WERE BORN FREE

Our inner wisdom can never be damaged, lost or broken. If you take nothing else with you after reading this chapter, take this sentence with you, write it down, put it somewhere where you can see it many times a day and LET IT SINK IN. Your body and mind are made to recognize truths.

Not only your inner wisdom can never be damaged, lost or broken. It is in you and everyone else, it is a constant, reliable, and a totally predictable system. This system carries a bunch of features that are universal, they work the same for everyone. YOU carry features that are unique to you, and they were given to you for you to take your place in this world and fulfil your purpose.

Welcome to my world. I am Vanessa and with this story I wish to inspire my readers to really see the treasure that they are RIGHT NOW, to see the several truths that can be found in one place and to know that their inner God always knows... every single one of us was born free.

I am 45 years old, and my life today is the result of me listening to my inner guidance and wisdom and guess what!? I too, learned this the hard way and that is totally ok! If you are struggling, know that in every struggle there is a hidden treasure and that in every moment there is a choice, to guide you in every choice there is an inner compass, a question you can ask yourself when your inner wisdom has been covered by the inner parrot in your head and your attachment to things or people being a certain way takes over. The question is: Am I seeing things from freedom or from judgement?

Today, I am a healthy, happy, and free human being, exactly what I was born to be. I do what I love, and I live in abundance of all kinds, most of all an abundance of love and freedom. I am nowhere close the place I want to be, and I am totally fine with it because I have FINALLY understood that I was never lost, even when I thought I was and therefore, I am positive I will arrive at my destination, although at this point, I am only concentrating on the journey.

It took me half my life to be fine with the present moment, to be fine with the way things went and to be fine, having absolutely no idea where I am headed because I know now that the God in me knows.

You may have heard this before. we, you were born with everything you need to fulfil your destiny on this planet. Nothing is too high up, too difficult, or out of reach for you. NOTHING!

I was born in a catholic country with a highly patriarchal structure and a dictator that ruled for 40 years. In fact, I was born just two weeks after he passed away. For you to get an idea of what the country was like at that point, only one language was allowed in spoken and written form, in case you do not know, in Spain there are three other languages in use besides Spanish. Women were meant for cooking and caring for children, men were meant to work and dictate what the rest of the family should do. Children were told to be quiet and stay away from trouble. Fixing problems was for professionals, just hospitals and house doctors available, the old natural medicine had been put on hold for a while. People were requested to be at home at 10 in the evening, or else, they could end up in jail.

And so, my story starts as if two parallel worlds existed beside each other and I could just alternate my existence between the two.

Imagine a child that at an incredibly early age, had an opinion, a strong opinion about everything. A child that from an early age did things that freaked (nearly) everybody out. A little two-year-old natural born leader. Imagine that child in the above country and culture! Imagine the contrast!

Surreal but true. Outside the house, I spent lots of time alone. I did not have many friends because I felt that the games the kids of my age played were boring and stupid. I sat down and observed people. I asked myself questions about God. I thought of all the trouble in the world and tried to find solutions. I wanted to change things. Outside the house I was the leader, inside the house, I was the: 'I wish I were different so I would not have to fight for my room to be who I am.' The conflict was born.

At home I felt restricted and misunderstood. According to my family I was too difficult, opinionated, too fast, impertinent. I wanted to grow up too fast. I wanted things my older sister had never asked for. I had to lie to get my way. I disappointed my parents, especially my mother. I felt so sad, so misunderstood, so lonely. At home, I felt so alone that I carried a Bible around. My family was not practicing religion, but it was somewhat present in our lives. That Bible to me represented my connection with God and so I talked directly to him. The bible represented the channel, the talking and the praying were my place of comfort. I never heard a reply, but I knew deep inside me that I was being heard.

The struggle within myself was real, by the time I reached my 17th birthday I was depressed not only because of this but because in my loneliness and feeling of having to stand on my own, I sought comfort in relationships, these relationships ended up always in tears. This only made me feel more inadequate and wrong about myself. The situation escalated when the one person I let deep inside my life, betrayed me. He was my boyfriend at the time, a deeply wounded young man that was also looking to comfort himself by having several relationships at once. Long story short, I ended up in the hospital, almost losing my life. I came out of this experience totally broken, I felt worthless, and I wondered what I was in this life for. I cried myself to sleep most nights. I spent a lot of time alone thinking and despite the pain and as incredible as it may sound, the story between us did not end there. This wounded soul would be in my life for another two years. The worst two years of my life.

This was the turning point for me.

In this outer and absolute misery, trapped with this relationship and away from my family, I realized that the feeling of inadequacy creeps into everyone at some point in life. Seriously, I do not know anyone who has not felt off, lonely, abandoned, an outcast, an outsider at some point in their life, starting in their early years. There is always the conflict between the individual and the collective, the attributes you were born with to fulfil your destiny and the rules, regulations and expectations that favourite the group.

I started to really think about who I was and what I was going to be doing with my life. I realized I had taken on a relationship to avoid family restrictions and what I encounter was ten times worse. How ironic! During that time, I realized I had been born to live my life. No one could live it for me. I broke with the sick relationship, with the past, the common friends, and places. I moved in with my brother and his wife. Forever grateful they took me in their home. Now I had changed the rules in the game, I had the chance to take full responsibility for myself.

Taking responsibility for myself meant that it was my duty to see, to see who I was, what my qualities were and how I was going to make the right choices, to live my life for myself. It also meant that I needed to become conscious of all the patterns and restrictions I had taken on to myself. Every one of us, learn from the people around us and we take on societal restrictions that come along with culture. These societal restrictions are the most difficult of all because we learn them and carry them unconsciously. I clashed with my family because certain things I was obviously were shaking the status quo. I ran away from that only to encounter the same, freedom was in me, not in the circumstances I was choosing. Today, I believe the reason I was born there is exactly because I needed to!! In a place where everything was restricted, limited, dictated, and boxed, not to say, jailed. The rebel energy of breaking free was needed, the leader to show them, they could do differently was needed.

This is the truth I was not seeing. I was there to teach others to be more reactive, to have stronger opinions, to act. I was bringing it what I naturally had. I was in the right place at the right time, I just never realized it and that is why I struggled! So instead of seeing this truth. I felt inadequate, stupid, like an outcast. I felt I so restricted. I felt I needed to fight for the right and the room to move and be me and all the while. I kept on judging myself because I was comparing myself to the people I had around me.

As human beings we have certain needs, and the biggest need we have is the feeling of belonging. When that feeling is threatened, we get into survival mode and start complying with things we do not want to comply to, and the inner conflict is born. The conflict between the individual and the collective.

Our minds fluctuate between feelings of awesomeness and worthlessness, courage and fear, action, and inertia, happy and unhappy. It is all human and it is all totally ok. No judgement. The fluctuation in our thought process can happen several times within one minute, it can happen differently depending on the subject, some situations trigger us more than others but at the end, the fluctuation is just an amazingly simple thing, it is a thought process that works the same way for everyone. We run away from this, looking for new places and new people, only to encounter what we run from all over again.

Our thought process feels like the ultimate truth to us because none of us can experience the world with someone else's senses. Our mind is a helpful tool, and it is always trying to be helpful. The thought process that follows in your head is never good or bad, it is just helpful or unhelpful, depending on what the base for the thought process is. If the thought process is, there is something wrong with me and I do not fit in here, I should be different, the result is a bunch of overthinking, judgement, and struggle. If the base for the thought is, I am awesomely unique, I am here to bring my gifts to the others and to fulfil my destiny by taking my place in the group or collective, the result will be, find a loving, easy, create way to do that. The mind will always deliver what we ask it for.

Realizing that every single person on this planet has a different set of features and natural skills within themselves to fulfil their destiny in this life and realizing that the key to happiness is to find these gifts and see how you can serve the world with them, is probably the quickest way to break free from the bunch of societal constraints and collective beliefs we live attached to. We all have our place.

And so, this is how I came back to myself and things got rolling.

First, I realized my life was about me, not about the others. My life, my responsibility. I felt stronger than ever! And then...

I started getting severe recurrent bronchial infections (got to be kidding me, right!?) After almost dying from a bad reaction to antibiotics, I decided I was never, ever going to use prescription drugs again. I realized medication was not the solution as I recognized the root cause of those infections was not some bacterium, it was the grief I felt for the stuff I had gone through for two years. I had never dealt with it and my body was letting me know. More awareness coming my way!

Here is where I learned that a crisis is a gift in disguise. Being recurrently ill was not funny but had I not had that adverse reaction to antibiotics, I would have maybe not made that decision so quickly and radically, although I had been drawn to natural medicine all my life. This period of continuous illness also allowed me to spend more time at my parent's place, they lived 110 kms away from the city. During one of those times, I went out with a friend a met a young Dutch man that rocked my world. He was the kindest person I had ever met.

Again, I saw clearly how making strong decisions and naturally following the things that appealed to me put me into the flow of destiny.

Another such strong decision took me to the Netherlands at 21 years of age. In the first year in a foreign country, I learned more about myself that in the previous ten years altogether. Once there, I found that my fascination for foreign things was not a coincidence; I learned I was naturally good at learning foreign languages and so I learned Dutch in one year and became fluent in English, since I had the chance to speak it daily. Learning Dutch gave me the chance the get a job and so I did. I was working at an office and one Friday afternoon the CEO of the company invited us to have a glass of wine after work, this is quite common in the Netherlands, and I agreed to go. While we were talking this man asked me: What are your aspirations for the future? What would you love to do?

I answered: I have been fascinated with natural medicine for a long time. I would like to become a homeopath.

He said: Really? Do you know? In the city where I live, there is a naturopathy school. I will look up the name and the contact details and give it to you! Just another funny 'coincidence', right!?

One year later I applied to get in the academy to start my 6-year studies on Natural medicine and Homeopathy. This is how my path on natural healing modalities solidified, up until that point it was just something interesting that my grandmother had taught me a bit about. This was the moment that marked the first steps on this path and now twenty plus years later, I share my wisdom with the world.

Bits of wisdom for the journey.

All these years, through struggles and bouts of good luck I learned...

- It is always about YOU first!
- Any kind of restraints, societal or otherwise are only a restraint if we let them be. For me, the most difficult thing was not to break with outside restraints but to break with inside restraints.
- You are unique, you have unique gifts and a unique path.
- Being different to others is not a curse, is a necessity. Find your place in the group, according to your gifts. Use your gifts to live a fulfilled life.
- Judgement is human but it is not helpful. When in judgement forgive yourself and look for helpful thoughts of love. Remember your mind is a tool and is always trying to help you and it will always answer according to the question you are asking. Ask better questions!
- Even when you feel you have no idea where you are or what to do. Be ok with it!
- The GOD in you ALWAYS knows. Ask the questions and then listen.
- Go to the things your naturally drawn to, these are possibly related to your unique gifts and will most likely take you towards your unique path.
- Ultimately, you were born free, you just learned to cover your freedom with thought patterns and ideas. If you put them on, you can take them off.

The above realizations have helped me find the path of freedom, away from restraints, both personal and societal. I turned away from the labels that others put on me and the labels I put on myself. I trusted my gut, even when I was scared. I did struggle with my thoughts and my feelings, but I learned from all the situations, especially the hard ones and with all these experiences I concluded that happiness starts with freedom. You can not be a happy, fulfilled being unless you fully embrace who you are and do whatever you came here to do. Everyone is different, so embrace that and walk your unique path with courage! The God in you knows and your path ahead will be filled with blessings in many different forms. You can do it!

Healing comes from within, and wellbeing comes from freedom. Learn to understand your life's and your body's language of wisdom. You have it all within you.

Blessings to you goddess of courage.

Until we meet again...

Vanessa

ABOUT THE AUTHOR
VANESSA PARRADO

Vanessa Noemi is a homeopath, energy healer, entrepreneur, and published author that has thrived in the world of natural healing for 25 years. She is passionate about the body's own ability to heal and her life's work focuses on the mind-body connection and understanding the body's messages.

She inspires and guides her clients to take responsibility for their body and their life and teaches them to support their health and wellbeing with natural, chemical free, non-invasive, non-side-effect methods. She specializes in substance detoxes as these may impair the body's own ability to heal.

Her goal is to raise awareness on the limitless potential of self-healing and the freedom that comes from taking responsibility for one's health and life. Her motto is 'Wellbeing starts with freedom'. Freedom of choice leads to freedom of action which leads to freedom to live your best life, healthy, happy, and full of energy!

Vanessa Noemi was born in Barcelona, Spain and has lived abroad for 25 years. She speaks 5 languages fluently and loves the sea. Her passions to keep herself healthy and happy include wild swimming all year round, meditation, yoga, juicing and essential oils.

Website: *www.vanessanoemi.com*
Instagram: *https://www.instagram.com/vanessaenesencia*

Made in the USA
Monee, IL
19 August 2021